Help! I'm Leading a Children's Sermon

Help!

I'm Leading a

Children's Sermon

Volume One:
Advent to
Transfiguration
Sunday

by marcia
taylor thompson

SMYTH&HELWYS
PUBLISHING INCORPORATED · MACON GEORGIA

Smyth & Helwys Publishing, Inc.
6316 Peake Road
Macon, Georgia 31210-3960
1-800-747-3016

The paper used in this publication meets the minimum requirements of
American National Standard for Information Sciences—
Permanence of Paper for Printed Library Materials.
ANSI Z39.48–1984. (alk. paper)

Library of Congress Cataloging-in-Publication Data

Thompson, Marcia Taylor, 1963-
Help! I'm leading a children's sermon : ready-to-use,
follows the Christian year, over 70 sermons
by Marcia Taylor Thompson.
p. cm.
ISBN 978-1-57312-329-7
1. Bible—Children's sermons.
2. Church year sermons.
3. Sermons, American—21st century.
I. Title.
BS491.5 .T48 2003
252'.53—dc21

2002153758

Table of Contents

Common Lectionary Year C

Appendix

Preface

But when Jesus saw this, he was indignant and said to them, "Let the little children come to me; do not stop them; for it is to such as these that the kingdom of God belongs. Truly I tell you, whoever does not receive the kingdom of God as a little child will never enter it." And he took them up in his arms, laid his hands on them, and blessed them. (Mark 10:14-16)

Jesus recognized the importance of children and their trusting faith when he rebuked the disciples who wanted to turn the children away. Children are an important part of the kingdom, though we do not always treat them that way.

Children are a vital part of the worshiping community and need experiences that create a sense of belonging. Children's sermons provide this opportunity and should be events of proclamation. This book contains a collection of children's sermons based on the Common Lectionary Years A, B, and C from Advent to Transfiguration Sunday. They are intended to involve children creatively in worship and proclamation of the Word. You will find two sermons for each Sunday. Each emphasizes Scripture and includes key verse(s) to be read within the sermon. The goal of this book is to help you invite children to participate in corporate worship in a meaningful, creative way by asking questions and using hands-on activities to explain scriptural themes.

The introduction to each sermon lists the title, the Scripture, a key verse or verses, key concepts, and the preparation and materials that you will need for your time with the children. Unique features of these sermons are the use of a key verse or verses within the sermon and the Bible as a visible presence. It is my hope that those who proclaim God's love through children's sermons will focus on the importance of the Bible and the text within the sermon's framework. Another useful feature is the option of two sermons for every Sunday of each lectionary year, along with an appendix of sermons on topics important to the spiritual development of children. You will also want to note that the sermons are written in conversational language.

This book is above all a guide for you to create your own children's sermons. Because each of us has a unique style, the ways we invite the children to join us and the ways we close our time with the children will differ. I encourage you to find your own pattern for your time together. Use these sermons as a beginning point and adjust them in the way that you think will be meaningful for the children in your church. It is important to take time to get to know the children so that you can engage them more fully in this time of proclamation.

Be aware that involving children in the sermon is always risky. Be ready for the unexpected. Often the unexpected enables a more vibrant proclamation of God's Word that is very real for the children (and adults also).

Remember that your primary focus is the children who come forward to participate. There are, however, other children and adults of the congregation who will also be listening and watching. They may even laugh at some of the dialogue. Their reactions let you know they are listening, but do not let them become your focus.

Be cautious in making generalized statements unless you know they are true for all your children in the congregation. For example, you would not want to talk about how all mothers are loving if you know a child in your church has been abandoned. Generalized statements can hurt feelings and create a barrier where children feel that they do not belong and their relationship with you is in jeopardy.

Make sure that as you use sermons with props, you try to include all the children if possible. Make a list of the children you have chosen so that you can remember from week to week which individuals have had an opportunity. There are often a few enthusiastic children who will volunteer for everything. Try to find ways to involve those who sit in the back or are a little shy.

Be creative, spontaneous, and flexible as you spend this important proclamation time with children. Be yourself. Children know when someone is genuine and concerned about them. Take this opportunity to share the good news of God's love and saving grace with the children. They have been entrusted to us and we have a great responsibility to help them grow in faith.

As you prepare for your time with children, let this be your prayer: *Let the words of my mouth and the meditation of my heart be acceptable to you, O Lord, my rock and my redeemer.* (Psalm 19:14) Amen.

Common Lectionary
Year A

First Sunday of Advent

Title: Will Peace Ever Come?

Scripture: Isaiah 2:1-5

Key Verse: [God] shall judge between the nations, and shall arbitrate for many peoples; they shall beat their swords into plowshares and their spears into pruning hooks; nation shall not lift up sword against nation; neither shall they learn war any more. (Isaiah 2:4)

Key Concepts: God's peace, God's presence

Materials: Bible, information about unrest in the world, globe or map to show place of unrest

Preparation: Read current information about war and unrest in some part of the world. Prepare to share the situation as simply as possible with the children.

(Begin this sermon by telling the children as simply as you can about unrest/war in some location of the world. If possible, have a globe or map to show the place you talk about.)

Do you think there will ever be peace in this place? *(Let the children respond.)* Maybe if the people who are fighting talk to each other, they might create peace. Sometimes peace doesn't come until one side wins the war and has the power to tell the people they were fighting what to do. But is that really peace?

How will peace ever come? The prophet Isaiah told the people of God long ago about how peace will come. The people of God had been fighting and had lost their city, Jerusalem. They longed to have their city back and for peace to come again. Isaiah told them that when God's presence was the focus of all people, peace would be known. All people would come to God's house and learn God's ways. *(Open Bible.)* Isaiah 2:4 says, *[God] shall judge between the nations, and shall arbitrate for many peoples; they shall beat their swords into plowshares and their spears into pruning hooks; nation shall not lift up sword against nation; neither shall they learn war any more.* Isaiah was telling God's people that when peace comes, all people will turn their weapons into tools to be useful in farming. The swords were to be made into plowshares to till the soil, like a hoe. The spears were to be made into pruning hooks to clear and trim vines. God's people wouldn't need weapons because there would be no more war.

As we prepare for the coming of Jesus during this Advent season, let us keep our minds focused on God. Let God teach us God's ways. May we spread God's peace. Let us pray for *(the people in your current event)*, that they may seek God's presence so that peace can come for them.

First Sunday of Advent

Title: Putting On Jesus

Scripture: Romans 13:11-14

Key Verse: Instead, put on the Lord Jesus Christ. (Romans 13:14a)

Key Concepts: Christian discipleship, salvation

*Materials: Bible, oversized dress-up clothes of specific characters or
occupations*

I need one boy and one girl volunteer to put on these clothes. *(Choose two
volunteers and give them the clothes to put on. As they put on the clothes, ask the
other children the questions that follow.)* While [child's name] and [child's
name] are dressing up, let's talk about the clothes we wear. What are the different types of clothing you put on each day? *(Let the children answer until
the volunteers finish dressing.)* Now, [child's name] and [child's name] are
dressed up. Who do you think they look like? *(Let the children respond.)*

We can see that [child's name] is dressed up like [name of occupation or
character] and [child's name] is dressed up like [name of occupation or char-
acter]. What would they look like if they put on Jesus? *(Let the children
respond. Depending on age/maturity, you may have to help them. Open Bible to
Romans.)* In our Scripture lesson from Romans 13, Paul tells the church to
live honorable lives, for salvation is nearer than ever. Paul was telling them
that Jesus is coming! They were to *put on the Lord Jesus Christ* instead of just
doing what they wanted to do. They were to be like Jesus.

As we enter this Advent season of eager waiting, Jesus is coming and salvation is nearer than ever for us. We're to live as disciples of Jesus, putting on
characteristics of love, justice, and peace. We're to try to be like Jesus so that
when others see us and the way we live they will know we belong to Jesus.
We're to put on Jesus every day. So when we get up in the morning, we need
to put on Jesus!

Second Sunday of Advent

Title: Preparing for Jesus

Scripture: Matthew 3:1-12

Key Verse: "Repent, for the kingdom of heaven has come near." (Matthew 3:2)

Key Concepts: Repentance, sin, preparation

Materials: Bible, biblical attire

Preparation: Ask an adult volunteer to play the role of John the Baptist and recite the monologue below.

We do many things to get ready for Christmas at our house. We get ready by decorating. We write Christmas cards to send to family and friends. We prepare for parties. We buy and wrap gifts to share with loved ones and friends. But is that all the preparing we should do? Advent is a time of preparing for Jesus' coming. How do we get ready for Jesus? *(Now the adult playing John the Baptist should enter, saying the key verse.)*

Monologue

Repent, for the kingdom of heaven has come near. Repent, for the kingdom of heaven has come near. For those of you who don't know me, my name is John the Baptist. I'm sort of an odd guy. I wear strange clothes, I live in the wilderness, and I eat bugs and wild honey. But I have an important message to bring to you just as I did long ago. To prepare for Jesus, it's important that we confess our sin—that means telling God those things we have done that we know aren't pleasing to God. When we confess our sin, repentance can begin. Repentance is more than just telling what we've done wrong. It means that our actions will change. And the exciting news is that Jesus is coming, so prepare. *(John the Baptist exits.)*

(Conclude time together.) John the Baptist told us how we can begin to prepare for Jesus. *(Open Bible to Matthew 3.) Repent, for the kingdom of heaven has come near.* Let's get ready.

Second Sunday of Advent

Title: Welcomed by Jesus!

Scripture: Romans 15:4-13

Key Verse: Welcome one another, therefore, just as Christ has welcomed you, for the glory of God. (Romans 15:7)

Key Concepts: Sharing the good news, welcoming others

Materials: Bible

Welcome! *(Pause)* Have you ever thought about what it means to be welcomed? The word welcome can mean pleasant, agreeable, pleasing, or nice. So when we welcome others, we're saying it's nice or pleasing to us that they're with us.

I want us to take a moment now to welcome each other, including the grown-ups. *(Start the welcoming. Give everyone a chance to mingle and welcome for about a minute, and then move toward settling the children again to finish your time together.)*

It feels good to welcome others and to be welcomed. *(Open Bible to Romans 15.)* Paul wrote in Romans 15:7, *Welcome one another, therefore, just as Christ has welcomed you, for the glory of God.*

It's important as followers of Jesus to remember to welcome others because Jesus welcomed everyone. The good news of Jesus is for all people. We're to welcome people as a way of praising God. This is important for us to think about during this Advent season. Jesus is coming, welcoming us to be his followers. Let's welcome others by sharing the good news that Jesus is coming.

Third Sunday of Advent

Title: Seeing Differently
Scripture: Psalm 146:5-10
Key Verse: The Lord opens the eyes of the blind. (Psalm 146:8a)
Key Concepts: Praise, God's presence, God's help
Materials: Bible, binoculars

Today, I brought a pair of binoculars with me for us to look through. Let's look at the (name an object). *(Pick an object in the sanctuary. Focus the binoculars so that the object is clear. Have the children come up one at a time to look at the object through the binoculars.)* It can be fun to look at things with binoculars. Let's try one more. *(This time, pick an object but do not focus the binoculars clearly. Again, have the children come one by one to look at the object. They may say they cannot see it or it isn't clear. Give each child a chance to view the blurry object.)*

It seemed that most of you had a hard time seeing the second object, and you were right. The binoculars weren't in focus, which means we couldn't see [name of object] clearly. It was hard to see. *(Pause)* Our Scripture lesson from Psalm 146 tells about seeing differently. *(Open Bible to Psalm 146.)* Psalm 146:8a says, *The Lord opens the eyes of the blind.* We know that God healed people who couldn't see with their eyes. There's another type of blindness, though. This blindness happens when people don't understand what God wants from God's people. Sometimes we don't understand things clearly, like looking through binoculars that aren't focused. It doesn't make sense to us. God can help us see things differently when we put our trust and focus on God. We can look to the past and see all that we've learned about God. We know there's still much more to learn.

You might wonder what this has to do with Advent and Jesus' birth and coming. Here's something for all of us to think about as we prepare for Jesus. From what you've learned about preparing and celebrating Jesus' coming, how will you prepare and celebrate differently? Do you see things differently? Can your celebration and preparation be the same as it was last year? These are questions that we can all prayerfully consider as we continue to worship together.

7

Third Sunday of Advent

Title: Patient Promise

Scripture: James 5:7-10

Key Verses: Be patient, therefore, beloved, until the coming of the Lord. The farmer waits for the precious crop from the earth, being patient with it until it receives the early and late rains. You also must be patient. Strengthen your hearts, for the coming of the Lord is near. (James 5:7-8)

Key Concepts: God's faithfulness, patience

Materials: Bible

What are some days during the year that are hard to wait for? *(Let the children respond—you may get answers like Christmas, birthdays, the last day of school, etc.)* These days are hard to wait for, but they always come. We celebrate Christmas every December 25th. Each of you has a special day when you were born, and you celebrate that day each year. It can be hard to wait for these days. When we want them to happen *now*, some people may say that we don't have patience.

In our Scripture lesson, James calls for patience. *(Open Bible to James.)* James 5:7-8 says, *Be patient, therefore, beloved, until the coming of the Lord. The farmer waits for the precious crop from the earth, being patient with it until it receives the early and late rains. You also must be patient. Strengthen your hearts, for the coming of the Lord is near.* In Bible lands, they had a dry season and a rainy season. The farmer was sure of this pattern and planted the crops at the right time so they could harvest food to eat. James was sure of the Lord's coming. James knew that God was faithful to God's promises.

During this Advent season, as we prepare to celebrate the coming of the baby Jesus in the manger, we can be sure of the promise. The coming of the Lord is near. We are to be patient and ready, for it will happen.

Fourth Sunday of Advent

Title: Announcing Jesus

Scripture: Matthew 1:18-25

Key Verses: Now the birth of Jesus the Messiah took place in this way. (Matthew 1:18a)

"She will bear a son, and you are to name him Jesus, for he will save his people from their sins." (Matthew 1:21)

"Look, the virgin shall conceive and bear a son, and they shall name him Emmanuel," which means, "God is with us." (Matthew 1:23)

Key Concept: Jesus' identity

Materials: Bible, three birth announcements

Preparation: Prepare three birth announcements for the Christ child. Use medium-sized posterboard pieces. Write "Messiah" on the first piece, "Jesus" on the second, and "Emmanuel" on the third.

We're getting close to celebrating the birth of Jesus. Christmas is only [number of days] days away. Many times when people have a baby, they send out birth announcements to their family and friends. Today I brought several birth announcements for baby Jesus. Let's look at this one. *(Hold up the announcement that has "Messiah" as the name.)* What's the name on this announcement? *(Let the children respond. Open your Bible.)* In Matthew 1:18 we read, *Now the birth of Jesus the Messiah took place in this way.* To call Jesus the Messiah tells us a lot about who Jesus is. He's the one who brings salvation, who heals our relationship to God.

Let's look at another announcement we could send out for baby Jesus. *(Hold up the announcement that has "Jesus" as the name.)* What's the name on this announcment? *(Let the children respond.)* In Matthew 1:21, the gospel writer tells us what "Jesus" means. It says, *"She will bear a son, and you are to name him Jesus, for he will save his people from their sins."* Jesus is the one who will save us from our sins—the things that we do wrong against God's way.

Let's look at the last announcement. *(Hold up the announcement with the name "Emmanuel.")* What's the name on this announcement? *(Let the children respond.)* Matthew 1:23 says, *"Look, the virgin shall conceive and bear a son, and they shall name him Emmanuel," which means "God is with us."* This name tells us that Jesus will always be with us forever.

As we prepare to celebrate Jesus' birth, think about what Matthew has told us about Jesus. Jesus is the one who heals our relationship to God by saving us from our sins. Jesus is with us forever. What a special birth announcement. Thank you, God, for your Son Jesus. Amen.

Fourth Sunday of Advent

Title: I Belong to Jesus

Scripture: Romans 1:1-7

Key Verse: . . . including yourselves who are called to belong to Jesus Christ. (Romans 1:6)

Key Concepts: Chosen, calling

Materials: Bible, two sets of four pictures, instant camera, film, photographer

Preparation: Gather two sets of four pictures. Three pictures in each set should have something in common; one doesn't belong. (For example, provide three photos of boys and one of a girl.) Also, ask an adult to take an instant picture of your group as you play your matching game.

(Ask an adult to take an instant picture of the group playing the game to use later in the sermon. Instruct him/her to take the picture as soon as the group assembles.) This morning, I want us to play a simple game. I brought some pictures for us to see. I also need four volunteers to hold them up. *(Choose the volunteers and give them the first set of pictures to hold.)* Isn't it nice to be chosen to do something? Now look at these four pictures. Which picture doesn't belong? *(Let the children answer.)* Here's another set of pictures. *(Give the volunteers the second set of pictures to hold.)* Which picture doesn't belong to the group? *(Let the children answer. You may want to elaborate on why the picture does not belong.)*

[Photographer's name] took a picture of us while we were playing the game. Let's look at our picture. Who doesn't belong? *(Let the children answer. Be prepared for some possible creative answers.)* That was a tricky question because we all belong. What we have in common is that we belong to Jesus. In the beginning of his letter to the Roman church, Paul told how he was chosen by God to bring the good news of Jesus. *(Open Bible to Romans 1.)* In Romans 1:6, Paul told the followers of Jesus that they also *are called to belong to Jesus Christ.* To be chosen or to belong makes us feel special. How special it is to celebrate the birth of Jesus! How special it is to belong to Jesus' family!

First Sunday after Christmas

Title: Praise God Who Makes Us and Saves Us
Scripture: Psalm 148

Key Verse: [God] has raised up a horn [of salvation] for his people, praise for all his faithful, for the people of Israel who are close to him. Praise the Lord! (Psalm 148:14)

Key Concepts: Praise, creation, salvation

Materials: Bible

Does anyone remember or know the story of creation from Genesis? *(Let some of the children answer. You may get a variety of answers, so be prepared to guide the discussion of creation in the direction you want to go.)* Many of you have told me the things God created. In fact, if we look at the story in the book of Genesis, God spoke and those things you shared were created.

Our Psalm lesson for today is praise for God. All of creation is praising God. The sea creatures, the snow, the wind, the mountains, the hills, the fruit trees, the wild animals, the birds, kings, princes, young men and women—all are praising God, because God created them. But that isn't all. The God who creates is also the God who saves. *(Open Bible.)* Psalm 148:14 says, *[God] has raised up a horn [of salvation] for his people, praise for all his faithful, for the people of Israel who are close to him. Praise the LORD!* The writer of this Psalm was full of praise and thankfulness to God. The psalm writer knew that God had created Israel and had saved Israel. You know some of the stories, such as the one about the Israelites being led out of Egypt by Moses. *(You can add other examples if you like.)* God saved God's people over and over again.

Like the psalmist, we can praise God who made us and who saves. What joy we have in celebrating the birth of Jesus who brings us a new beginning. Praise the Lord!

First Sunday after Christmas

Title: *Jesus Can Help Us*

Scripture: *Hebrews 2:10-18*

Key Verse: *Because [Jesus] himself was tested by what he suffered, he is able to help those who are being tested. (Hebrews 2:18)*

Key Concept: *Temptation*

Materials: *Bible, Christmas cookies or candy for each child*

Preparation: *Ahead of time, enlist one child to sneak and eat their cookie or candy.*

Today I brought some Christmas cookies/candy for each of you. There's only one thing I'm going to ask you to do after I give it to you. You can't eat it, okay? *(The children may voice their displeasure at this time. Go ahead and give them their cookie or candy.)* Now everyone has a cookie/piece of candy. What do you think we should do with them since we can't eat them? *(Children may express that eating would be a good thing to do. Have the child you enlisted sneak a bite. The other children will either join in, or they will tell on the person who ate.)*

I told [child's name] to sneak a bite of cookie/candy. You may all eat your cookie/candy when you return to your seats. How hard is it not to eat something you want to eat? It can be difficult. When we want to do something we're not supposed to do, we call it a temptation. There are many things that can tempt us or test us.

The good news is that Jesus can help us when we are tempted or tested. *(Open Bible.)* Hebrews 2:18 says, *Because [Jesus] himself was tested by what he suffered, he is able to help those who are being tested.* There are times when it can be hard to do what Jesus wants us to do. We're tempted to do things that may not please Jesus. But we need to remember that Jesus knows how hard it can be for us and can help us as we try to be his followers. Through Bible study and prayer, Jesus can help us when we're tempted or tested.

First Sunday after Epiphany

Title: New Things

Scripture: Isaiah 42:1-9

Key Verse: See, the former things have come to pass, and new things I now declare; before they spring forth, I tell you of them. (Isaiah 42:9)

Key Concept: God's power

Materials: Bible, old dirty pennies, vinegar, salt, jar, paper towels (include one moistened with water), bowl

Today we're going to see if we can get these old dirty pennies clean. First let me try this. I'm going to yell at the pennies and see if they will come clean. *(Put them in your hands and yell at the pennies.)* "Be clean, pennies!" Did it work? *(Let the children respond—of course not.)* Now let's try a wet paper towel. Would [child's name] like to try and clean the pennies? *(Let a child try to rub the pennies clean. Though they may remove some dirt, the pennies still won't shine.)* Let's try one more thing. I brought a jar of vinegar mixed with salt. Let's put the pennies in the jar and shake them around. *(Place the pennies in the jar.)* Now, let's take the pennies out of the jar. *(Pour the pennies into a bowl. Then take them out of the bowl and wipe them with a paper towel.)* Yes, we did get the old dirty pennies to look new again.

God can do new things with us. *(Open Bible.)* Isaiah 42:9 says, *See the former things have come to pass, and new things I now declare; before they spring forth, I tell you of them.* God can and will do new things by God's Spirit working through each of us. Just like we used vinegar and salt to clean the pennies, God can work in us as we help others. We can share the story of Jesus when we visit the sick, make cards for shut-ins, or just enjoy time with our friends. As we do these things and many others, God's love and power working through us can make a difference in the lives of other people. It can make them new.

First Sunday after Epiphany

Title: God's Impartiality

Scripture: Acts 10:34-43

Key Verses: "I truly understand that God shows no partiality, but in every nation anyone who fears him and does what is right is acceptable to him." (Acts 10:34b-35)

Key Concept: God's acceptance of all

Materials: Bible, basketball, baseball, carrot, green beans, bag

(You may use pictures of foods, objects, or events if you prefer. This is written using the actual items.) I brought a bag full of things for us to look at today. Let me pull out a couple of items. *(Pull out the carrots and green beans.)* I have carrots and green beans. My favorite between these two vegetables is green beans. Now raise your hands to answer. Who like carrots best? *(Let the children raise hands.)* Who likes green beans best? *(Let the children raise hands.)* It looks like more people like [vegetable] than [vegetable]. We might say this group is partial to [vegetable]. To be partial to something means that we like it more.

Let's try another pair of items. *(Pull out the basketball and baseball.)* Here I have a basketball and a baseball. Now, I like both of these sports, but I like basketball just a little more than baseball. You might say I'm partial to basketball because I like it more than baseball. Now all those who like basketball more than baseball raise your hands. *(Let the children respond.)* All those who like baseball more than basketball raise your hands. *(Let the children respond.)* It looks like this group is more partial to [sport] than to [sport].

We all have foods or games we like better than others. It can even be that way with our friends. We may like one friend better than another, and that's okay. Usually those are the friends who like the things we like. But isn't it wonderful to know that God loves and accepts each of us? *(Open Bible.)* In Acts 10:34-35, Peter says, *"I truly understand that God shows no partiality, but in every nation anyone who fears him and does what is right is acceptable to him."*

In the early church, there were Jewish Christians and Gentile Christians. At first, there was an argument about whether the Gentiles could be part of the church. Peter had a dream from God that helped him understand that

God's love was for everyone through Jesus. It's a wonderful feeling to know that we're loved and accepted by God. God shows no partiality. That means God cares for all of us equally.

Second Sunday after Epiphany

Title: You Can't Keep Jesus

Scripture: John 1:29-42

Key Verse: "And I myself have seen and have testified that this is the Son of God." (John 1:34)

Key Concept: Telling others about Jesus

Materials: Bible

Raise your hand if you've ever seen or experienced anything exciting that you could tell us about this morning. *(Choose two or three children to share their exciting event with the group. You may have to bring closure by commenting that it's easy to talk about exciting things.)* It's easy for us to talk about exciting things we have seen. When we see something exciting, we want to tell everyone—our parents, our friends, and sometimes even people we don't really know.

In our Scripture lesson, John the Baptist had seen Jesus. *(Open Bible.)* In John 1:34 John says, *"And I myself have seen and have testified that this is the Son of God."* John was so excited about seeing Jesus that he had to tell others, or *testify* as the Scripture tells us, that Jesus was the Son of God. John the Baptist saw Jesus in person. We see and learn about Jesus through studying the Bible, through mission projects, and through prayer—just to name a few ways. When we "see" Jesus or learn about Jesus, we shouldn't keep it to ourselves. We should be just as excited or even more excited than we were about the things we shared this morning. We should be so excited about Jesus that, like John the Baptist, we share the good news with others. Jesus is the Son of God!

Second Sunday after Epiphany

Title: The Fellowship of Jesus

Scripture: 1 Corinthians 1:1-9

Key Verse: God is faithful; by him you were called into the fellowship of his Son, Jesus Christ our Lord. (1 Corinthians 1:9)

Key Concept: Community

Materials: Bible, building blocks

Today I'm going to give each of you a block. After I give you the blocks, I want you to work together to build a pyramid. *(Let the children build their pyramid. Commend the children for working well together.)* Now that you've built the pyramid, how would you feel if someone came and knocked it down? *(Knock it down quickly and get the children's reaction. They will probably voice their complaint. Try to regain order and continue.)*

As you built the pyramid together, you worked as a group. Another group that works together is our church family. The group of people of our church could be called a "fellowship." *(Open Bible.)* Long ago, Paul wrote to the church fellowship in Corinth and said, *God is faithful; by him you were called into the fellowship of his Son, Jesus Christ our Lord.* He told this group of people they were called by God to be a community of Jesus Christ. That means each person must work to help the group be a community of Jesus Christ.

How do we do that? We encourage each other during difficult times. We make sure that our choices are the best for everyone and not just for ourselves. We help each other by discussing the Bible and praying for each other. We do things together that make others feel happy, like being a friend and thanking them for their help. I was not a good helper when I knocked down your pyramid.

People in a good community work together to help each other. We do everything we can to be like Jesus. What we do each day shows what our church is like. Our actions need to show that we're a part of the group that's like Jesus.

Third Sunday after Epiphany

Title: "Peek-a-Boo"

Scripture: Psalm 27:1, 4-9

Key Verses: "Come," my heart says, "seek his face!" Your face, Lord, do I seek. Do not hide your face from me. (Psalm 27:8-9a)

Key Concept: God's presence

Materials: Bible, baby and parent

Preparation: Invite a parent to bring their infant to participate in your time with the children. Ask them to play peek-a-boo with the baby before you begin.

(If you choose to have a baby participate in your sermon, ask the baby's parent to play peek-a-boo with the baby before you begin. The following is written as if you didn't choose this option. Adapt accordingly.)

Have you ever played peek-a-boo with a baby? When you play, you hide your eyes and then say "peek-a-boo." Babies enjoy this game. Did you know that this game helps babies learn something? *(Let children respond.)* When babies are small, the only things they know are there are the things they can see. You'd know that if I left the sanctuary, I was in another room or place. A baby wouldn't know that. Playing peek-a-boo helps babies learn that things and people are there even though they can't always see them. It's also a fun face game because it seems to surprise and excite them.

I think it would be nice to see God's face. Do you wonder what God looks like? *(Let the children respond.)* The psalmist who wrote Psalm 27 was seeking God's face just like a baby wants to see our face when we play peek-a-boo. Psalm 27:8-9a says, *"Come," my heart says, "seek his face!" Your face, LORD, do I seek. Do not hide your face from me.* The writer knew that God heard this prayer. Even though the psalmist couldn't see God's face physically, he or she knew that God was there. At the end of the psalm the writer says that we must *wait for the LORD.* Maybe it will be sort of like that peek-a-boo surprise. When we study the Scriptures or pray, we may feel God's with us in a very surprising and exciting way. What's most important, though, is to seek God's way in all we do or say so that other people will know we're God's children.

Third Sunday after Epiphany

Title: *Instant Commitment*

Scripture: *Matthew 4:12-23*

Key Verses: *And he said to them, "Follow me, and I will make you fish for people." Immediately they left their nets and followed him. (Matthew 4:19-20)*

Key Concepts: *Christian commitment, discipleship*

Materials: *Bible*

(If desired, you can make this sermon more specific by picking one child's parent as the example. Adjust the sermon to make it accurate for the person you choose.)

What would you think or say if your parent came home and told you they quit their job because Jesus had something new for them to do? Now remember, this means they won't make any money to buy food or pay other bills. What would you think? *(Let the children respond one at a time. You may get various responses. Guide the children accordingly.)* If my husband came home and told me that, I'd be shocked and probably angry. How could he leave me with the responsibility of feeding and raising three children on my own? I'd be really worried. Most of us wouldn't think about the fact that *Jesus* asked the person to do something else.

This happens in our Scripture lesson. *(Open Bible.)* In Matthew 4:12-23, we learn about Jesus' beginning his ministry by calling four of the disciples. These followers happened to be fishermen. This was their job. This trade helped them pay their bills and buy food to eat. Verses 19-20 are the shocking part of the story. They say, *And he said to them, "Follow me, and I will make you fish for people." Immediately they left their nets and followed him.* They were fishing for fish one day and fishing for people right after they met Jesus. They left their job and their family behind because Jesus called them to come. It must have been scary, yet we know that they instantly accepted Jesus' call to follow him.

As Jesus calls us, we need to be ready. Sometimes it may mean taking risks. It may mean that others don't always accept you at school or in other groups. If we choose to follow Jesus' call, Jesus expects total commitment to him. That can be hard, but through prayer Jesus will help us.

Fourth Sunday after Epiphany

Title: Not Stuff

Scripture: Micah 6:1-8

Key Verse: He has told you, O mortal, what is good; and what does the Lord require of you but to do justice, and to love kindness, and to walk humbly with your God? (Micah 6:8)

Key Concepts: Trust, justice, covenant

Materials: Bible

I want to ask you an important question, and then I want you to raise your hand if you would like to answer. If you could pick out one special thing to give to God, what would it be? *(Call on the children who raise their hands. You will probably get a variety of answers. Some may be close to the key concepts, while others may be far from it. Accept every answer as valid.)*

In Old Testament times, God's people, the Israelites, weren't sure about what God wanted from them. *(Open Bible.)* In our Old Testament lesson from the book of Micah, the Israelites thought God wanted their stuff like burnt offerings, rams, oil, or even their firstborn children. But God didn't want their stuff. What God wanted is found in Micah 6:8, which says, *He has told you, O mortal, what is good; and what does the Lord require of you but to do justice, and to love kindness, and to walk humbly with your God?* That's what God wants from us!

Let's break this down into smaller pieces so we can understand. First, God wants us to do justice. To do justice means to be fair and not to take advantage of someone else. Second, God wants us to show loving kindness in our relationships with other people by doing what is good for them. Another way of saying this is that we're to live in covenant with God and each other. And last, we're to walk humbly with God. This means we're to trust God daily and act the way God wants us to in all that we do. These are the three special things God wants from us.

Fourth Sunday after Epiphany

Title: True Happiness

Scripture: Matthew 5:1-12

*Key Verses: "Blessed are those who mourn, for they will be comforted. . . .
Blessed are the peacemakers, for they will be called children of God."
(Matthew 5:4, 9)*

Key Concept: True happiness

Materials: Bible, chart paper, marker, easel (optional)

Preparation: Write on the chart paper "I'm happy when . . ."

How would you finish this sentence if I said "I'm happy when . . ."? Think about how you would answer while I get my chart paper and marker ready. *(Get out your materials.)* Now raise your hand and I'll call on you. *(Select a child to respond and continue until all who want to answer have had a chance. Write down their responses on the chart paper, summarizing as needed.)* We have an interesting list of things that would make us happy.

Did you know that Jesus told his followers how they could be happy God's way? *(Open Bible.)* In Matthew 5:1-12, Jesus taught his followers using what we call the Beatitudes. The Beatitudes can be called attitudes that are pleasing to God. For example, Matthew 5:9 says, *"Blessed are the peacemakers, for they will be called children of God."* So when we work to make peace happen, we're happy and blessed. This is an attitude that's pleasing to God.

Another way to have an attitude that pleases God is to say a word of encouragement and hope to someone. For example, Matthew 5:4 says, *"Blessed are those who mourn, for they will be comforted."* When somebody has lost something or someone important to them, they're sad. This beatitude says that God will comfort them.

We can think of many things that will make us happy, but true happiness and blessing come when we live as God wants us to live. The Beatitudes give us a guide to know how to live. They also give us words of encouragement and hope.

Fifth Sunday after Epiphany

Title: Fearing and Following God

Scripture: Psalm 112:1-9 (10)

Key Verse: Praise the Lord! Happy are those who fear the Lord, who greatly delight in his commandments. (Psalm 112:1)

Key Concept: Fearing God

Materials: Bible

What do you fear the most? *(Let the children respond. Assist as needed with suggestions of scary things, such as being lost, being in the dark, or getting sick.)* All of you who shared your fears told of things that are scary or frightening to you. Fear is something we feel when we feel unsafe, alone, or hurt.

When I was your age and I heard Bible verses with the word "fear," they didn't make sense. *(Open Bible.)* Psalm 112:1 says, *Praise the LORD! Happy are those who fear the LORD, who greatly delight in his commandments.* It just doesn't make sense to be scared of God. Why would people be happy if they feared God? Just like a lot of words in our language, "fear" has another meaning. Fear can also mean reverence, awe, wonder, and worship. If you insert those words into the verse, it makes sense. God's so amazing. We can't begin to understand all that God is. Because of all the wonderful things God does for us and our world, we can be happy by fearing God and following God's commandments. Let's fear and follow together.

Fifth Sunday after Epiphany

Title: Flavor and Light

Scripture: Matthew 5:13-20

Key Verses: "You are the salt of the earth; but if salt has lost its taste, how can its saltiness be restored? It is no longer good for anything, but is thrown out and trampled under foot. You are the light of the world. A city built on a hill cannot be hid. No one after lighting a lamp puts it under the bushel basket, but on the lampstand, and it gives light to all in the house. In the same way, let your light shine before others, so that they may see your good works and give glory to your Father in heaven." (Matthew 5:13-16)

Key Concept: Daily witness

Materials: Bible, salted and unsalted potato chips, flashlight, basket, bowls

I brought with me two bowls of different kinds of potato chips. I want you to try this bowl first. *(Let children taste the unsalted chips first.)* Now I want you to compare them with this bowl of chips. *(Let them taste the salty chips.)* Which chips had more flavor? *(Let the children respond. Most will say the second bowl has more flavor, but be prepared for someone to choose the unsalty chips.)* The second bowl had more taste, more flavor, because the chips had salt. The first bowl of chips didn't have salt.

I also brought a flashlight and this basket. *(Turn on the flashlight and put it under the basket so no light appears.)* Can you see the light? *(Children will hopefully say "No.")* Of course not. The light is hidden in the basket so you can't see it.

Did you know that Jesus used both salt and light to teach his disciples about their daily witness? Their daily witness was their actions before others. *(Open Bible.)* In Matthew 5:13-16, Jesus tells his disciples this: *"You are the salt of the earth; but if salt has lost its taste, how can its saltiness be restored? It is no longer good for anything, but is thrown out and trampled under foot. You are the light of the world. A city built on a hill cannot be hid. No one after lighting a lamp puts it under the bushel basket, but on the lampstand, and it gives light to all in the house. In the same way, let your light shine before others, so that they may see your good works and give glory to your Father in heaven."*

Jesus told his followers that they were to be full of flavor like salt. They were to stand out and show others what it meant to be followers of Jesus. They were to be like a light. *(Shine the flashlight into the room.)* The light goes on and on beyond what we can see. The disciples were to go out into the world to be a witness to the world of God's love and God's kingdom.

Like the first disciples, we're to be salt and light. Let's make an effort this week to be full of God's flavor and to be God's bright light to our community. We can help others know of God's love!

Sixth Sunday after Epiphany

Title: Choices

Scripture: Deuteronomy 30:15-20

**Key Verse: Choose life so that you and your descendants may live, loving the
Lord your God, obeying him, and holding fast to him. (Deuteronomy
30:19b-20a)**

Key Concept: Choices

Materials: Bible

What are some choices you make each day? *(Let the children respond to the
question. Assist as needed by suggesting that they pick out their clothes, brush
their teeth, eat, etc.)* We make many choices during the day. If you think
about it, everything we do involves a choice that we make. Sometimes we
make the right choices and sometimes we don't. When we make the wrong
choices, like not doing what a parent asks us to do, we sometimes get pun-
ished. Punishment is usually a sad and joyless time. No one is happy.

In the Old Testament, Moses told God's people before they entered the
promised land about a very important choice. The choice was whether they
would follow God's commandments or choose not to follow them. *(Open
Bible.)* Moses told the people this: *Choose life so that you and your descendants
may live, loving the* LORD *your God, obeying him, and holding fast to him.*

This is a daily choice we also have to make. We either choose to follow
God's way or our own way. Life God's way can bring joy and peace. When
we go our own way, we sometimes end up in trouble and there's no true happiness. As you get up each morning, say to yourself, "I choose to live God's
way today!" Then let your actions and choices show your love and obedience
to God.

Sixth Sunday after Epiphany

Title: Who Gives the Growth?

Scripture: 1 Corinthians 3:1-9

Key Verse: So neither the one who plants nor the one who waters is anything, but only God who gives the growth. (1 Corinthians 3:7)

Key Concept: God's power

Materials: Bible, seeds, pot with soil, watering can, water

Today I brought seeds, a pot of soil, and a watering can. I'd like you to help me plant the seeds so that we can have a beautiful plant. Who would like to volunteer to help? *(The children will raise their hands. Choose two or three children—one to plant the seed, one to hold the pot, and one to water. After the seed is planted and watered, let the children return to their places.)*

Now we're ready for the plant to grow. *(Hold the pot, look at the plant intensely, and forcefully speak to it.)* Grow! Plant, grow! Grow! Plant, grow! Did the plant grow yet? Do you see it coming out of the dirt? *(Children will say no and some may laugh.)*

I've heard that talking to plants will help them grow. What do you think our seeds need to grow? *(Let the children respond—water, soil, sunlight, time, etc.)* All these things are needed to help the plant to grow. But really, God's the one who makes it grow. God created the seed and all that it needs to become a plant.

In one of his letters, Paul told the Christians in Corinth that God is the one who grows their faith. Some of the people were arguing about which leaders had helped them to know more about Jesus. Paul used the plant as a way to tell them that God is the one who makes their faith grow. *(Open Bible.)* In 1 Corinthians 3:7, Paul writes, *So neither the one who plants nor the one who waters is anything, but only God who gives the growth.* Paul wanted the Christians of Corinth to know that church leaders didn't make their faith grow; God did. The different leaders helped their faith grow just like we can help a plant by giving it water, soil, and sunlight, but the growth comes from God.

You have different leaders who help you grow so that you know more about Jesus. Your parents, Sunday school teachers, mission leaders, and even I help you grow as we teach you about Jesus. We all want you to grow to know and love God more each day. We may help guide you toward God, but remember, God is the one who loves you and made you and helps you grow in faith.

Seventh Sunday after Epiphany

Title: Reflecting God

Scripture: Matthew 5:38-48

Key Verse: Be perfect, therefore, as your heavenly Father is perfect. (Matthew 5:48)

Key Concept: Reflecting God's character

Materials: Bible, hand mirror

I brought a mirror with me today. I want each of you to look in the mirror and tell me what you see. *(Start passing the mirror around. Have each child tell who they see by saying their name. Be prepared for them to giggle or laugh a bit.)* When you look in the mirror, you can see yourself. It's called a reflection. The way the mirror, the light, and your eyes work helps you see this reflection. All of you said that you saw yourself when you looked in the mirror. How you look in the mirror is how other people see you.

Did you know that I see something else when I look at each of you? I see a gift from God. God wants us to follow God and do those things that God would do. *(Open Bible.)* That's why in Matthew 5:48, Jesus says, *Be perfect, therefore, as your heavenly Father is perfect.* Being perfect like God means that in all we do and say, we reflect God's way. We're to act the way God acts. That means the way we treat others should be the way God would treat them. It may mean being nice to someone you don't particularly like out of your love for God and that person. It may mean being generous and sharing with others. We can't be perfect like God, but we should try to act the way God acts. So when we look in the mirror, we should see more that just [name] or [name]. We should see God's ways in us. Then others will see God, too.

Seventh Sunday after Epiphany

Title: Christian Builders

Scripture: 1 Corinthians 3:10-11, 16-23

Key Verses: Each builder must choose with care how to build on it [the foundation]. For no one can lay any foundation other than the one that has been laid; that foundation is Jesus Christ.
(1 Corinthians 3:10b-11)

Key Concept: Christian discipleship

Materials: Bible

(If your feet are small, then use someone with large feet as an example.) I remember when I was growing up how my feet got big before the rest of my body grew. I remember complaining to my mom about how my Sunday shoes hurt my feet. My parents took me to the mall to get some new shoes and they were surprised. I went from a size 4 to a size 8. I remember my grandfather and other people saying, "She sure has a good foundation." Has anybody ever said that to you about your feet? Well, what they meant was that my big feet would hold me up. They were good support for my body.

We all need another important foundation in our lives to hold us up and give us support. That foundation is Jesus. It's our responsibility as parents, teachers, mission leaders, deacons, and laity to help you come to know Jesus Christ. We want to help you learn more and more about Jesus and his love for you. Paul used the example of a foundation when he wrote to the Christians in Corinth, *Each builder must choose with care how to build on it [the foundation]. For no one can lay any foundation other that the one that has been laid; that foundation is Jesus Christ.*

You can also help another person come to know Jesus and help lay this special foundation. By your actions you can show others Jesus' love. What are some ways you can show others Jesus' love? *(Let the children respond. Affirm their answers in your response.)* You can invite friends to Sunday school, worship, and other church activities. You can read the Bible or look at pictures of Bible stories with a friend. By doing these things and other things you've said, you can be a Christian builder. You can make Jesus the foundation to hold you and others up.

Eighth Sunday after Epiphany

Title: Hopeful Trust

Scripture: Psalm 131

Key Verse: O Israel, hope in the Lord from this time on and forevermore. (Psalm 131:3)

Key Concept: Trust

Materials: Bible, a sturdy chair, blindfold

Preparation: Enlist five adults to help with the trust fall.

Today I need a really brave volunteer. Who would like to help? *(Let the children raise their hands. Choose a male if possible, since girls may be wearing dresses.)* Okay, [child's name], come be my helper. To be my helper today, I need you to wear this blindfold. *(Place the blindfold on the child. Cue the adult volunteers to come forward.)* I'm going to guide you over to this chair and I'll help you stand up on the chair. *(Have the adults line up on each side and one at the end of the chair. Have one person hold the hand of the child in the chair to make sure he/she will not fall.)* Now I want you to trust me and do what I tell you. I want you to fall backward out of the chair. *(At this point you may get some resistance from your brave volunteer. Give them a way out if they are truly scared. Make sure the adults are ready.)* You'll be caught, trust me. Now we're all going to count to three and I want you to lay back as it you were falling on your bed. 1-2-3, fall. *(The child may or may not fall—they may or may not trust you. Adjust the rest of the sermon according to what they do.)*

Trusting can be very hard when you can't see what's going to happen next. Our lives are that way, too. Sometimes it's easier to trust in ourselves or other people or things than to put our trust in God. All during Epiphany season, we have been learning and talking about God's power in our lives and how we should live differently. When we trust in God's power, we live differently. The writer of Psalm 131 knew this. *(Open Bible and read all of Psalm 131.)*

This is a song of trust. The psalmist says he doesn't let things take over his life but quietly comes before God in hopeful trust. We also need to come quietly before God in hopeful trust each day. We know that God is faithful to us and loves us. God will care for us. We just have to trust.

Eighth Sunday after Epiphany

Title: Come the Kingdom

Scripture: Matthew 6:24-34

Key Verse: "But strive first for the kingdom of God and his righteousness, and all these things will be given you as well." (Matthew 6:33)

Key Concepts: God's power, God's kingdom

Materials: Bible

When I was your age, my Sunday school teacher introduced me to a game called "Come the Kingdom." Now I want you to listen carefully so you can play the game. This game is a word game where you add to the end of the phrase "come the kingdom." The kingdom we're talking about is God's kingdom. From what we learn about God through Jesus, we can have an idea of what God's kingdom is like. To play the game, you think of something that you think God wants in God's kingdom. For example, "come the kingdom everyone will love each other." Would someone else like to try? *(Give the children a chance to respond. You may want to help them think of things they know about Jesus or things Jesus said. You might allow the congregation to participate as well.)*

In Matthew 6:33, Jesus said to his followers, *"But strive first for the kingdom of God and his righteousness, and all these things will be given you as well."* Jesus told his followers they didn't need to worry about things like food, clothes, or money, because when you worry about things you sometimes forget about God. He used an example of the birds. They have plenty to eat because God provides for them. Jesus tells us to work toward God's kingdom. We should work toward peace, love, and justice. We should not worry about things. God's power is great and God will provide what we need.

Transfiguration Sunday

Title: *Remember, But Don't Tell?*

Scripture: *Matthew 17:1-9*

Key Verse: *As they were coming down the mountain, Jesus ordered them, "Tell no one about the vision until after the Son of Man has been raised from the dead." (Matthew 17:9)*

Key Concepts: *Transfiguration, understanding*

Materials: *Bible*

Today is Transfiguration Sunday. On this Sunday, we read in our Scripture lesson about how Jesus took Peter, James, and John and went up on a high mountain. Right before the disciples' eyes, Jesus transfigured. *Transfigure* is a big word. It means changed. So Jesus changed right before their eyes. The Gospel of Matthew says that Jesus' face shone like the sun and his clothes became "dazzling white." Jesus was talking with Moses and Elijah. When this happened, the disciples were afraid. They didn't understand what they were seeing. Then it was over and they walked back down the mountain with Jesus. *(Open Bible.)* Matthew 17:9 says, *As they were coming down the mountain, Jesus ordered them, "Tell no one about the vision until after the Son of Man has been raised from the dead."*

Jesus told them to remember but not to tell people until later. The disciples didn't know that Jesus would be killed and then raised from the dead. They probably didn't understand what Jesus even told them. They might even have thought to themselves that no one would believe them anyway. People might think they were crazy. But they remembered and later understood what Jesus said.

Sometimes we understand what we see, hear, or experience only later. There are some things we hear about God or Jesus that don't quite make sense to us. Jesus' transfiguration may be one of those things. But if we continue to listen and watch and learn more and more about Jesus, we will have new understanding about Jesus and what it means to be one of his followers. This is true for you and for all of us. Just because I'm older doesn't mean I understand everything. I come to new understandings as I try to live as Jesus wants me to live. You can, too!

Transfiguration Sunday

Title: Coming Soon

Scripture: 2 Peter 1:16-21

*Key Verse: For we did not follow cleverly devised myths when we made
known to you the power and coming of our Lord Jesus Christ, but we
had been eyewitnesses of his majesty. (2 Peter 1:16)*

Key Concept: Transfiguration, Jesus' coming

Materials: Bible

How many of you have seen a movie at the theater? *(Let the children respond
by raising their hands.)* Before the movie starts, you see previews of movies
that are coming soon. The previews show us just a "little" piece of the movie
to catch our attention and make us want to come and see it. Previews give us
a view of the movies that are to come.

In our Scripture lesson from 2 Peter, we're reminded of the transfiguration of Jesus as a sneak preview of what's to come. The transfiguration of
Jesus took place when Jesus took Peter, James, and John and went up on a
mountain. Jesus changed right before their eyes. Jesus was shining like the
sun and he was talking with Moses and Elijah. These disciples saw a preview.
At first they didn't understand, but 2 Peter 1:16 says, *For we did not follow
cleverly devised myths when we made known to you the power and coming of our
Lord Jesus Christ, but we had been eyewitnesses of his majesty.* The transfiguration was a preview of Jesus' second coming. We only have what the disciples
have told us. We don't have a complete picture of what it will be like when
Jesus comes again. The transfiguration story is a view of what is to come—
Jesus. The disciples share this preview with us to catch our attention and to
make us want to come and see.

Common Lectionary
Year B

First Sunday of Advent

Title: Mold Me, Lord!

Scripture: Isaiah 64:1-9

Key Verse: Yet, O Lord, you are our Father; we are the clay, and you are our potter; we are all the work of your hand. (Isaiah 64:8)

Key Concept: God made us and can still create in us.

Materials: Bible, a small ball of clay for each child

(Give each child a small ball of clay.) Take your ball of clay and see what you can make out of it. I'll give you about a minute. *(Create something from clay along with the children. Carefully watch and see if any children start to make something and then pack their clay into a ball to begin again.)* What did you make? *(Give the children an opportunity to answer.)* Did any of you decide to change your clay creation after you started? *(You may get various responses.)* Clay is a substance that can be changed as long as it hasn't hardened or been baked. If you've ever seen a potter at work on a potter's wheel, the potter spins the wheel fast and uses his or her hands to create pottery out of clay. If the potter doesn't like a pot, he or she can change it.

We can think of God as a potter and each one of us as God's clay. God has made us and can keep making us. A long time ago, God's chosen people found themselves captive in a foreign land. Their enemies had destroyed their homes and their place of worship. They called to God in prayer. They trusted that God would help them if they followed God's laws and commands. *(Open your Bible to Isaiah.)* In the middle of hard times they called to God with these words found in Isaiah 64:8: *Yet, O Lord, you are our Father, we are the clay, and your are our potter; we are all the work of your hand.*

God's people knew they were not perfect. They waited with hope. They knew God would come to them and mold them. As we prepare for the coming of Jesus during this Advent season, let's be ready for God to come and change us. Let's let God mold us into what God wants us to be.

First Sunday of Advent

Title: Is It Time?

Scripture: Mark 13:24-37

Key Verse: Beware, keep alert; for you do not know when the time will come. (Mark 13:33)

Key Concept: God's presence and hope

Materials: Bible, alarm clock with loud alarm

Preparation: (Optional) Enlist an adult helper to set off the alarm clock.

(Set the alarm clock in an area where the alarm can be heard distinctly. You may even want to ask another adult to help you by setting off the alarm just as the children are coming forward.) What's that noise? *(You may get various answers, including the right one. Ask one of the children to find the alarm clock.)* The noise we heard was from an alarm clock. Why do you use an alarm clock? *(Let the children answer.)* We use an alarm clock to wake us up in the morning. Some people use alarm clocks to remind them of something important they're supposed to do. What happens if you hit the "snooze" button of the alarm or turn off the alarm without paying attention to it? *(Let children answer if they choose.)* If we ignore the alarm, we might be late for work or school. We would have to rush to get ready and sometimes we might not have the chance to get ready like we should.

(Open your Bible to Mark 13.) In Mark 13:33, Jesus told his disciples to *Beware, keep alert; for you do not know when the time will come.* Jesus was referring to his time of suffering, but also to the promise that he would come again.

Advent is a time of waiting and watching. It's a time of waiting for the birth of Jesus and knowing that through Jesus, God is with us. It's also a time of hope and promise that Jesus will come again. We don't know the time. We do know that Jesus has called us to be his disciples. Jesus wants us to be alert and ready. Through studying the Bible and prayer we can begin to prepare ourselves. God promises that we will never be left alone or without hope, for Jesus is coming soon.

Second Sunday of Advent

Title: *Echoing the Good News*

Scripture: *Isaiah 40:1-11*

Key Verse: *Get you up to a high mountain, O Zion, herald of good tidings; lift up your voice with strength, O Jerusalem, herald of good tidings, lift it up, do not fear; say to the cities of Judah, "Here is your God!" (Isaiah 40:9)*

Key Concept: *Tell others of Jesus' birth.*

Materials: *Bible*

Preparation: *Ahead of time, ask the choir director and choir to help you sing "Go Tell It on the Mountain" with the children.*

Have you ever heard an echo? *(Let the children answer briefly.)* An echo is a repeating of sound caused by reflection of sound waves. In other words, the sounds you make bounce off other things and you hear the sound repeated. A long time ago, God's people had been taken captive. The prophet Isaiah told them God was with them and would help them return to their land. *(Open Bible to Isaiah 40.)* In the book of Isaiah, the prophet tells the people to get up high on a mountain and shout, *"Here is your God!"* (v. 9) so all the people can hear. It would be amazing to have thousands of people shouting from the mountaintop. Think of how the sound would echo. What good news it was for God's people!

Today, I want us to echo some good news. Our organist/pianist is going to play through the chorus of "Go Tell It On the Mountain" while the choir sings. Then you'll help make good news by echoing what the choir sings. *(Let the choir sing the chorus once all the way through, then sing a second time and have the children echo each of the four phrases.)*

During this Advent season, take time to share the good news of Christmas—Jesus Christ is born. Share it with your friends and family. Let others know how important it is that Jesus is coming.

Second Sunday of Advent

Title: Messengers of God

Scripture: Mark 1:1-8

Key Verse: "See, I am sending my messenger ahead of you, who will prepare your way . . . ." (Mark 1:2b)

Key Concept: Tell the good news of Jesus.

Materials: Bible, Christmas card, cell phone, e-mail message printout

We get or give messages in many ways. What are some of the ways we give or get messages? *(Let children give answers.)*

A message tells us something. If I called your house with this cell phone *(pull out the phone)* and you have an answering machine, then I'd leave you a message to call me. Another way *(pull out e-mail message)* I might send you a message is through the computer. If you have an e-mail address, then I could type a message on my computer and send it to your computer. During this Advent season, if I sent you a Christmas card *(pull out Christmas card)*, I'd be sending you a happy message wishing you a Merry Christmas. Even the way we look sends messages or news of what's happening to us or around us. If I sat here with my arms crossed and a frown on my face, I'd be sending you a message that I was sad.

In our Scripture reading, we hear of a messenger who was sent a long time ago. *(Open your Bible to Mark 1.)* Mark 1:2 says, *"See, I am sending my messenger ahead of you, who will prepare your way . . . ."* The messenger was John the Baptist. He brought good news to people that the Savior, Jesus, was coming. We also need to tell this good news. During this time that we celebrate the birth of Jesus, we need to remember and remind others that Jesus loves us all and is our Savior. That's what makes a Merry Christmas. We can be God's messengers today by telling others about Jesus.

Third Sunday of Advent

Title: Be Rejoicers

Scripture: Psalm 126

Key Verse: The Lord has done great things for us, and we rejoiced. (Psalm 126:3)

Key Concepts: Gladness/sadness; rejoicing over what God has done and will do; hope

Materials: Bible, two paper plates

Preparation: Draw a happy face on one plate and a sad face on the other plate.

(Show the children the happy face plate.) What kind of face does this plate person have? *(Let children answer.)* What makes you happy or glad? *(Children will give a variety of answers. Move on as necessary.)* What kind of face does this plate person have? *(Show the children the sad face plate. Let them answer accordingly.)* What makes you feel sad? *(Let the children answer.)*

In the Old Testament, there is a book called Psalms. Psalms is a book of poems that were used as songs to worship God. Today we will read Psalm 126. This was a song that God's chosen people, the Israelites, sang as a prayer for God to help them. They remembered what God had done for them in the past and were glad. *(Open your Bible to Psalm 126.)* In Psalm 126:3, they sang, *The LORD has done great things for us, and we rejoiced.* God's chosen people also had times of trouble, and they cried tears when they were sad, but they always remembered God's goodness to them and had hope of shouting for joy because of what God would do for them in the future.

When we gather together for worship, we're rejoicers. We praise God and rejoice during this Advent season because God sent Jesus as our Savior. We're glad that Jesus has come. By meeting together with others at church, we learn about Jesus' birth, his life on earth, and his death and resurrection. God has given us so much to remember. As rejoicers, we're to share our reason for gladness with others.

Third Sunday of Advent

Title: Always Worshiping

Scripture: 1 Thessalonians 5:16-24

Key Verses: Rejoice always, pray without ceasing, give thanks in all circumstances; for this is the will of God in Christ Jesus for you. (1 Thessalonians 5:16-18)

Key Concept: We worship God every day in all that we do.

Materials: Bible

When we gather as a church family each Sunday, we rejoice together by singing hymns of praise to God. We just sang [hymn name] as a way to praise God. We spend time each Sunday morning in prayer. We pray for ourselves, for other people, and for our church. We give thanks to God for all God has done for us by coming together for this special time of worship. Is this the only time and place we can worship God? *(Let the children respond, realizing that answers may vary. You may get "yes" or "no" depending on the age and understanding of the children.)*

We can find the answer to my question in the Bible. *(Open Bible to 1 Thessalonians.)* In the New Testament book called 1 Thessalonians, Paul, a follower of Jesus, told the church of Thessalonica in chapter 5, verses 16-18: *Rejoice always, pray without ceasing, give thanks in all circumstances; for this is the will of God in Christ Jesus for you.* Paul's instructions were to rejoice always. This means we're to have joy and happiness because of God all the time. To pray without ceasing means that all we do, say, and think should be a prayer to God all the time. Giving thanks no matter what happens means that even when we're faced with hard or sad times, we should still thank God for all that God has done.

Paul's lesson for the church of Thessalonica and for us is that everything we do is to be an act of worship toward God. Sometimes we might try to separate our lives and only include God in certain areas. As we prepare to celebrate Jesus' birth, we should rejoice, pray, and thank God in all that we do, say, and think.

Fourth Sunday of Advent

Title: That's Impossible

Scripture: Luke 1:26-38

Key Verse: "For nothing will be impossible with God." (Luke 1:37)

Key Concept: With God, all things are possible.

Materials: Bible, two sheets of paper

Preparation: Write "possible" on one sheet of paper and "impossible" on the other.

Today I want to give you a test. I will give you the answers that you can choose from, but first I need two volunteers. *(Choose children that you know will be helpful. Give the "possible" sign to one child and the "impossible" sign to the other child.)* [Child's name] and [child's name] have the words needed to answer the test. The words are possible and impossible. If something is possible, we know it can happen. For example, a kitten comes from a mother cat. If something is impossible, we know it can't happen. For example, an alligator can't come from a chicken egg. Now you're ready for the test. [Child's name] and [child's name] will hold up the sign that you choose as the answer.

Questions: Is it possible or impossible that...

(1) A goldfish can live on land?
(2) A banana grows on a tree?
(3) A chicken can write a book?
(4) A dog can read the newspaper?
(5) An apple can be made into applesauce?

The things that were impossible sound silly! A chicken can't write a book; that's silly nonsense. *(Open Bible.)* But in our Scripture lesson from Luke 1:37, we find this verse: *"For nothing will be impossible with God."* Mary had a visit from the angel Gabriel, who told her that she would have a son by the Holy Spirit. Mary wondered how could this be possible. Her sister Elizabeth, who was too old to have children, was pregnant and she wondered how this could be. Mary learned from the angel that through God, all things are possible even when they seem impossible. As we prepare for Jesus' birth in the manger, think about how many stories you know in which what seemed impossible became possible with God. Think about how Jesus healed the sick and made enough food for five thousand people from a small lunch. Think about how this little baby Jesus has changed the lives of many people. Jesus came, died, and rose from the dead to forgive the sins and bring eternal life for all people who believe in him. Remember, with God, all things are possible.

Fourth Sunday of Advent

Title: Upside Down

Scripture: Luke 1:47-55

Key Verses: "My soul magnifies the Lord, and my spirit rejoices in God my Savior." (Luke 1:46b-47)

Key Concept: God's care and power will turn things upside down.

Materials: Bible, pillow

Preparation: (Optional) Ahead of time, enlist a male volunteer to stand on his head.

Today I need a volunteer to do something special for me. I need someone who will get upside down by standing on your head on this pillow I brought. I'll help you keep your balance. *(Choose a child who is willing, or your previously enlisted volunteer.)* [Child's name] is going to get an upside-down view of our congregation and sanctuary and describe it for us. *(Let the child who is upside down describe what he sees from this new perspective. Give him clues if he has difficulty. Can he see faces or feet, etc.? Let the volunteer return to an upright position.)* Now we'll let [child's name] describe the congregation and sanctuary from a regular view. *(Let the volunteer describe what he sees now that he is right side up.)*

In our Scripture lesson today, Mary sings a song of praise to God after she learns how God will use her as God's servant. *(Open Bible.)* In Luke 1:46b-47, Mary sings, *"My soul magnifies the Lord, and my spirit rejoices in God my Savior."* In Mary's song, she tells of how God's mercy will bring down the powerful and lift up the poor. The hungry will be fed and the rich sent away. Everything would be turned upside down by God's mercy and power through Jesus, God's Son. Just as [child's name] gave us a different description of the congregation and sanctuary than we expected, God's way was different from what the people expected their Messiah to be. Jesus would be a king who didn't seek power and riches, but a king who helped the poor, hungry, and helpless.

Today, we can sing with Mary and be God's servants. We praise God, who can turn the world upside down.

First Sunday after Christmas

Title: Praising God

Scripture: Psalm 148

Key Verse: Let them praise the name of the Lord, for his name alone is exalted; his glory is above earth and heaven. (Psalm 148:13)

Key Concept: All creation is to praise God.

Materials: Bible, large chart paper, marker

How many of you have seen "Blue's Clues" on television? *(Let children respond.)* For those of our congregation who don't know about "Blue's Clues," this is what happens. There's a dog named Blue and a person named Joe. On each episode, Joe tries to figure out something Blue wants to do by collecting Blue's clues. She marks her clues with paw prints. Today, we're going to solve a mystery. I need a volunteer to draw pictures of our clues on our big chart. *(Choose a child who is old enough to draw the pictures. Tell the child to draw simple outline pictures of the clues we find.)*

We have a mystery question. Who and or what is to praise the Lord? We're going to read from Psalm 148 and [child's name] will draw pictures of the clues we find in the Bible. I need you to listen carefully to who or what is to praise the Lord. When you hear something, raise your hand. *(Open your Bible and slowly read Psalm 148:1-12. You may want to read it in four-verse portions and then let your artist draw the clues from each portion. Let the children suggest the clues for your artist. Continue until you finish verse 12.)*

Look at all the pictures we have. Who and what are to praise the Lord? All of creation is to praise the Lord *for his name alone is exalted; his glory is above the earth and heaven* (v. 13). We've just celebrated the birth of Jesus. God loved us so much that God sent Jesus, and that's another reason to praise the Lord!

First Sunday after Christmas

Title: Grow in God's Favor

Scripture: Luke 2:22-40

Key Verse: The child grew and became strong, filled with wisdom; and the favor of God was upon him. (Luke 2:40)

Key Concept: Growing in God's favor

Materials: Bible, tape measure

When I was growing up, I always wanted to be taller. I constantly asked my mom or dad to measure me so I could see how tall I was. I wanted to grow and keep a record of my height. Do you ever wonder how tall you are? I brought a tape measure so we can find out how tall you have grown. *(Measure three or four children and emphasize how much they have grown.)*

Have you ever thought about what Jesus did when he was your age? In the Bible we only have one story about the boy Jesus at the temple. I've always wondered what Jesus liked to play or how he passed the time growing up in Nazareth. But there's something important we do know about Jesus from the book of Luke. *(Open Bible.)* Luke 2:40 says, *The child grew and became strong, filled with wisdom; and the favor of God was upon him.* Jesus grew up learning about God. We can do that, too. What can we do that will help us grow up in God's favor, learning all we can about God? *(Let the children respond. They may suggest reading the Bible, praying, attending Sunday school, reading Bible stories, helping others, etc.)* There are many things we can do to grow in God's favor. Let's ask God to help us grow up learning all we can about God.

First Sunday after Epiphany

Title: *God's Creation*

Scripture: *Genesis 1:1-5*

Key Verse: *Then God said, "Let there be light"; and there was light. (Genesis 1:3)*

Key Concepts: *God's creation, God's sovereignty*

Materials: *Bible*

Most of us are familiar with the creation story in Genesis. We've learned about all the things God created. Let's review and see how much you remember. *(For each day, pause to see it the children remember what was created.)* On the first day *(pause)*, God created light and made Day and Night. On the second day *(pause)*, God created the sky. On the third day *(pause)*, God created the seas, the dry land, trees, plants, and fruits. On the fourth day *(pause)*, God created the sun and the stars. On the fifth day *(pause)*, God created the fish and birds. On the sixth day *(pause)*, God created all the animals and people. On the seventh day *(pause)*, God rested.

Have you ever wondered how God made everything? Genesis 1:3 tells us how. *(Open Bible.) Then God said, "Let there be light"; and there was light.* God spoke the words and creation happened. It's amazing to think of God speaking to make all of creation come to life. This tells us something very important about God. God is the supreme, most excellent, free power. There's no one just like God. There's no one greater than God is. We call this *sovereignty.* When we say God is sovereign, we say that God is the most powerful being we know. We can see that in the beautiful creation God spoke into life. We can thank God for all of creation, and we should care for and protect this precious gift from God.

First Sunday after Epiphany

Title: Who Is Jesus?

Scripture: Mark 1:4-11

Key Verse: And a voice came from heaven, "You are my Son, the Beloved; with you I am well pleased." (Mark 1:11)

Key Concept: Jesus' identity as God's Son

Materials: Bible

Did you know that each of the first four New Testament books about Jesus' life begin differently? We call these four books the Gospels. The Gospels tell about the life and ministry of Jesus. Matthew begins his story about Jesus using a family tree. Then he tells the story of Jesus' birth. Luke begins by telling the story of the birth of John the Baptist and Jesus. John begins by telling who Jesus is, but there is no real story about Jesus' birth. Mark begins with John baptizing Jesus. There's no story of Jesus' birth or childhood. In Mark, we find Jesus as a young man ready to begin his ministry. This is our Gospel lesson for today.

It isn't surprising that we find differences in each of the Gospels. They're different because different people saw and wrote down what they learned from Jesus. If I asked each of you to write a story about what you learned and saw today at church, your stories would be similar, but not the same. Mark wanted to tell his readers right from the start who Jesus was. Twice in today's reading, Mark tells us that Jesus is God's Son. *(Open Bible to Mark 1.)* Mark 1:1 says, *The beginning of the good news of Jesus Christ, the Son of God.* And during Jesus' baptism, Mark 1:11 says, *And a voice came from heaven, "You are my Son, the Beloved; with you I am well pleased."*

It's special for Mark to let us know who Jesus is. When Mark writes that Jesus is God's Son, we know that this person is very special. We know that God sent us a special person to show us how to live each day. Jesus can show us the way to act and live and love.

HELP! I'M LEADING A CHILDREN'S SERMON: YEAR B

Second Sunday after Epiphany

Title: Did You Hear?

Scripture: 1 Samuel 3:1-10 (11-20)

Key Verse: Now the Lord came and stood there, calling as before, "Samuel! Samuel!" And Samuel said, "Speak, for your servant is listening." (1 Samuel 3:10)

Key Concepts: Listening to God and obeying God

Materials: Bible

I want us to play a simple game this morning. It's a listening game. I will whisper a sentence to [name of a child that is close to you] and then [same child's name] will whisper the same sentence to [the name of the next child closest to him/her]. There is a special rule. You can only say the sentence to the person three times. We will keep whispering the sentence until everyone has heard it. We're going to check and see what good listeners we can be. Let's start the game. *(Use the second portion of the key verse as your sentence: "Speak for your servant is listening." Once everyone has heard the sentence, ask the last person what he or she heard.)*

Now that everyone has heard the sentence, we'll let [child's name who was last to receive the message] tell us what he/she heard. *(Depending on the size of the group, the sentence may be correct or incorrect. Be ready for either response.)*

Sometimes it can be hard to listen, or we can't hear clearly what someone is saying to us. *(Open Bible.)* The sentence I said was from 1 Samuel 3:10: *Now the Lord came and stood there, calling as before, "Samuel! Samuel!" And Samuel said, "Speak for your servant is listening."* The story of Samuel is found in the Old Testament. Samuel was a young boy who grew up in the temple with the priest Eli. Samuel heard a voice, but at first he didn't know it was God. Eli helped Samuel and Samuel listened and obeyed God. We should also listen to God and be obedient. We may not hear a voice like Samuel did, but when we listen to others tell us about God, read our Bible, and pray, we need to listen to what God is telling us and obey what God wants us to do. It might be that God wants us to help another person, be a friend to a new person in school, do what our parents say, or share our toys. We can ask God to help us listen and obey.

49

Second Sunday after Epiphany

Title: Have You Seen?

Scripture: John 1:43-51

Key Verse: Jesus answered, "Do you believe because I told you that I saw you under the fig tree? You will see greater things than these." (John 1:50)

Key Concept: Accepting Jesus

Materials: Bible

Preparation: Contact several parents to find out specific characteristics about their children that stand out in their minds. Ask for characteristics that you would otherwise not know. Choose information that will not embarrass the child.

Did you know that . . . *(Fill in this portion with the things you learned about some of the children. They may ask how you know this information. At first, you may tell them you simply know. Eventually, tell them how you found out those specific things about them.)*

In our Scripture lesson, we have the story of Philip and Nathanael. They are called as disciples of Jesus. Nathanael's response to Jesus is special. Philip tells Nathanael about Jesus, but Nathanael doesn't think Jesus could be that great. Jesus comes from such a small town that doesn't seem important. Philip introduces Nathanael to Jesus anyway. Jesus tells Nathanael that he saw him under the fig tree before Philip called him. Nathanael doesn't know how Jesus knew that. He was all alone. Nathanael then believes and says he accepts Jesus as God's Son. *(Open Bible.)* In John 1:50, *Jesus answered, "Do you believe because I told you that I saw you under the fig tree? You will see greater things than these."* Nathanael believed and followed Jesus and did see greater things.

We learn about the life of Jesus through studying the Bible. What are some things we know that Jesus did? *(Let the children respond.)* Just as Philip and Nathanael had to decide whether to follow Jesus, we have to choose each day whether we'll accept and follow Jesus' way. If we choose to follow Jesus, we can ask him to help us do what is right and pleasing to him.

Third Sunday after Epiphany

Title: My Rock

Scripture: Psalm 62:5-12

Key Verse: He alone is my rock and my salvation, my fortress; I shall not be shaken. (Psalm 62:6)

Key Concepts: God's protection and care

Materials: Bible, a small rock for each child

Today I brought some rocks. I'd like for each of you to take one. *(Give time for the children to choose a rock.)* What do you know about rocks? How would you describe them? *(Let the children respond. Acknowledge and repeat the children's descriptions of the rocks.)* What do we do with rocks? *(Let the children respond.)* Rocks have many uses. They are strong.

(Open Bible.) Psalm 62:6 says, *He alone is my rock and my salvation, my fortress; I shall not be shaken.* What do you think the psalmist was writing about? *(Let the children respond.)* The psalmist wrote about God. The psalmist meant that God gives strength, salvation, and protection. God cares for each of us today and protects us. God gives us strength and should be the solid rock foundation for our lives. That means that we should look to God always in all that we do. Then when difficulties come our way, like the psalmist we will not be shaken. We will know that God cares for us in good times and bad times. We will find our strength by looking to God.

I want you to keep your rock in a place where you will see it often. Let it remind you that God is your rock, your guide for all of life.

Third Sunday after Epiphany

Title: *Turn Around Toward God*

Scripture: *Jonah 3:1-10*

Key Verse: *Human beings and animals shall be covered with sackcloth, and they shall cry mightily to God. All shall turn from their evil ways and from the violence that is in their hands. (Jonah 3:8)*

Key Concepts: *Repentance and forgiveness*

Materials: *Bible*

Has there ever been a time when something really nice happened to someone you don't like? *(Let the children answer, but avoid details.)* How did it make you feel when something nice happened to this person who may have acted mean or unfriendly? *(Let the children respond with words of emotions.)* It can make us mad when good things happen to people we think are mean, rude, or unfriendly to us.

Did you know that the prophet Jonah had the same problem? He didn't like the Ninevites at all. He thought they were wicked and violent, and he was right. God told Jonah to tell the city of Nineveh that they were doomed for their evil ways. Jonah was glad to do this, but something surprising happened. The king told all the people to turn to God in repentance. *(Open Bible.)* Jonah 3:8 says, *Human beings and animals shall be covered with sackcloth and they shall cry mightily to God. All shall turn from their evil ways and from the violence that is in their hands.* The people repented and God didn't destroy them. But this made Jonah mad. He thought God should punish the Ninevites for their evil ways. God was forgiving, but Jonah wasn't.

The word *repentance* means to turn around completely—180 degrees! *(Demonstrate by standing and turning 180 degrees.)* It means turning away from doing the things we know are wrong and turning toward God. None of us does what is right all the time, but it's good to know that our God loves us. God loves us so much that when we do wrong, we can turn toward God and ask for God's forgiveness.

Fourth Sunday after Epiphany

Title: Who Is a Prophet?

Scripture: Deuteronomy 18:15-20

Key Verse: I will raise up for them a prophet like you from among their own people; I will put my words in the mouth of the prophet, who shall speak to them everything that I command. (Deuteronomy 18:18)

Key Concept: Prophets can reveal God's purpose.

Materials: Bible, pictures of Martin Luther King Jr. and Mother Teresa

Did you know that God called many people to be prophets? A prophet was a person who spoke for God. A prophet's job was to tell God's message to the people. Usually the message was for the present time, but sometimes prophets told about the future. In the Old Testament, there were many prophets. Elijah and Elisha were prophets who did great things, but they didn't write down their prophecies. We only have stories of the things they did. Other prophets, such as Jeremiah, Isaiah, Hosea, and Malachi, wrote down their prophecies.

Deuteronomy 18:18 is a promise from God. *(Open Bible.)* In the time of Moses, God said, *I will raise up for them a prophet like you from among their own people; I will put my words in the mouth of the prophet, who shall speak to them everything that I command.* From the beginning, God promised to give the people a prophet who would bring God's word. Many of the prophets spoke words from God that people didn't want to hear. Often God's people didn't do what God told them to do through the prophets. They wouldn't listen.

Do you think God sends prophets today? *(Let the children respond.)* I have two pictures of people we might call prophets. Martin Luther King Jr. spoke prophetic words in his peaceful movement toward equality for all people. *(Show the picture and let the children share anything they know about King.)* Another prophet is Mother Teresa, who spoke and acted out of love and compassion to people who were dying and had no place to go. *(Show the picture.)*

(If you wish, share the names of other prophets familiar to your community.) God may want you to be a prophet and speak God's message to God's people. That's why it's important to listen and learn all that God has to teach us.

Fourth Sunday after Epiphany

Title: "Love-Them-Alls"

Scripture: 1 Corinthians 8:1-13

Key Verse: Knowledge puffs up, but love builds up. (1 Corinthians 8:1b)

Key Concept: Love for others builds community.

Materials: Bible, balloon

Don't mention names, just say yes or no. Have you ever met somebody who was a "know-it-all"? I've known some people like that. They have an answer for everything, and their answer is the only answer. Is it hard to be friends with a person like that? Why? *(Let the children respond. Expect various answers.)* Sometimes without knowing it, friends can make you feel bad because it seems that you're never right or your idea isn't right. Sometimes what you feel is important isn't important to them. Sometimes we even do this to our friends without noticing it.

In New Testament times, Christians at Corinth were having this same problem. They had disagreements over things they believed were important. *(Open Bible.)* In 1 Corinthians 8:1b, Paul wrote to the Corinthian church, *Knowledge puffs up, but love builds up.* I have a balloon. What will happen if I keep puffing and puffing? *(Start blowing up the balloon, but don't make it pop unless you think it will not frighten the children.)* If I keep puffing air into the balloon, it will pop. Paul meant that sometimes you have to give up some things for others because love is what builds community. It doesn't mean that you never stand up for what you believe in, but that every person in the community should be treated with love and respect.

In Sunday school or even when we gather here for our children's time, we need to let each person share his or her own answer or opinion without laughing or making the person feel bad. People sometimes have different opinions. In the activities you do together, make sure everyone is included, even if it's someone you don't like as much. God has called us to love so that we can make our church what God wants it to be. Instead of being "know-it-alls," let's be "love-them-alls."

Fifth Sunday after Epiphany

Title: Beyond Measure

Scripture: Psalm 147:1-11, 20c

Key Verse: Great is the Lord, and abundant in power; his understanding is beyond measure. (Psalm 147:5)

Key Concepts: God's understanding and care

Materials: Bible, yardstick, paper, pencil

Today I brought a yardstick so we can measure some things. *(Ask an older child to measure and a child who can write to record the measurements. Give each child the tools they need.)* First, I'd like [child's name] to measure the height of the pulpit. *(Give time for measurement and recording.)* Next, I'd like you to measure the length of the front pew. *(Measure and record.)* Now, I want you to measure the width of the doorway into the sanctuary. *(Measure and record.)* Last, I want you to measure how much love Mr. and Mrs. [name from your congregation who are sitting together] have for each other. *(At this point, the child may say he/she cannot measure this with a yardstick.)* You can't measure that with a yardstick? Well, can you measure how much strength Mr. [name of someone who looks strong] has? *(Pause)* You can't measure that, either. Come back to your seat and let's talk about this a bit more.

Some things are easy to measure. Things such as the door or the pulpit are objects that don't change. We can touch them. When I asked [child's name] to measure love between two people or the power someone has, measuring became much harder. These are things that we can't touch with our hands. *(Open Bible.)* In Psalm 147:5, we can learn about God's understanding. It says, *Great is the Lord, and abundant in power; his understanding is beyond measure.* God's understanding and God's care for us are so great that they can't be measured. It's great for us to know that God cares for us so much. It can help us when we're afraid or scared. It helps us all to know that we're loved so much by a great God. Remember this week in all that you do, God's understanding and care are beyond measure.

Fifth Sunday after Epiphany

Title: Expectations

Scripture: 1 Corinthians 9:16-23

Key Verse: . . . woe to me if I do not proclaim the gospel!
(1 Corinthians 9:16c)

Key Concept: The gospel is to be heard, enjoyed, lived, and preached.

Materials: Bible

Today we're going to talk about expectations. Expectations are what other people think we should do or what we think we should do. Your parents probably expect you to do certain things such as brushing your teeth and cleaning up your room. What else do your parents expect you to do? *(Give the children an opportunity to respond.)* Besides your parents, other people expect you to do certain things. Your teachers, coaches, and friends all have expectations of you.

Have you ever thought about what Jesus expects from you? Paul thought about this a lot. In New Testament times, Paul was a missionary and wrote many of the letters we find in the New Testament. *(Open Bible.)* In 1 Corinthians 9:16, Paul writes, . . . *woe to me if I do not proclaim the gospel!* Paul had a strong feeling that he should share the good news of Jesus with everyone he met. We should have that strong feeling, too. We should want to share the good news with all the people we see each day. What are some ways that we can tell the good news of Jesus to others? *(Let the children respond.)*

There are many ways that we can proclaim or tell the good news of Jesus to others. Jesus expects his followers to tell that news. The good news of Jesus is to be heard, enjoyed, lived, and preached so that others can know of Jesus' love. This is what Jesus expects of us.

Sixth Sunday after Epiphany

Title: I Choose

Scripture: Mark 1:40-45

Key Verse: Moved with pity, Jesus stretched out his hand and touched him, and said to him, "I do choose. Be made clean!" (Mark 1:41)

Key Concept: Accepting others

Materials: Bible

In our story from the Gospel of Mark, Jesus heals a man with leprosy. A man with leprosy comes to Jesus and asks if Jesus would choose to make him well. *(Open Bible.)* Mark 1:41 says, *Moved with pity, Jesus stretched out his hand and touched him, and said to him, "I do choose. Be made clean!"* Jesus healed many people. But Jesus did something else when he chose to heal this man. The disease of leprosy was a skin disease. In biblical times, the Jewish people believed that a person got leprosy because of the bad things they had done. People with leprosy were considered unclean by Jewish law. That means they were not accepted and often had to live away from family and friends. Nobody wanted to be around someone who had leprosy.

Who are some people that we don't accept? Can you think of people that you find very hard to accept and love? *(Let the children answer. Affirm their answers by repeating them.)* Sometimes we find it hard to accept people who are different from us. It may be that they have a different skin color, have a disease, or have no home. But Jesus shows us what our response needs to be. We're to love and accept those who are different from us, especially when they call to us in need. What are some ways we can choose to show God's love to people in need? *(Let the children answer. Suggest answers if needed.)* Jesus can use each one of us to help people who are in need feel the healing love of Jesus through our actions. I hope that each of you will choose to help others who may be different by accepting them and loving them through Jesus Christ.

Sixth Sunday after Epiphany

Title: The Real Race

Scripture: 1 Corinthians 9:24-27

Key Verse: Do you not know that in a race the runners all compete, but only one receives the prize? Run in such a way that you may win it. (1 Corinthians 9:24)

Key Concept: Discipleship

Materials: Bible, gold medal or blue ribbon, trophy, pair of running shoes

(Set out the pair of running shoes for the children to see.) Today, I brought running shoes. I need your help, though. If I put on these shoes to run a race, what would I need to do to make sure I win? *(Give the children an opportunity to respond to the question. Offer suggestions if needed.)* As I run around the racetrack, I have to run in the right direction and stay in my lane. What would happen if I didn't follow the rules? I would be out of the race with no chance to win. If I do all these things that we've just said, will I win for sure? If I win, I wonder what my prize would be? It could be a gold medal or a trophy. *(Show one of them.)*

(Open Bible.) In 1 Corinthians 9:24, Paul writes, *Do you not know that in a race the runners all compete, but only one receives the prize? Run in such a way that you may win it.* Sometimes in the Bible, the writers used everyday events to help people understand what it means to be a Christian. Paul used the event of a race to help people understand that it takes effort to be a disciple of Jesus. You have to practice it. You have to set goals such as reading your Bible and praying daily to keep on track. The prize at the end of this race is better than a trophy or a medal. It's God's kingdom. God's kingdom is wherever God is king. God's love will be found there forever.

Seventh Sunday after Epiphany

Title: Faithful Friends

Scripture: Mark 2:1-12

Key Verses: Then some people came, bringing to him a paralyzed man, carried by four of them. And when they could not bring him to Jesus because of the crowd, they removed the roof above him; and after having dug through it, they let down the mat on which the paralytic lay. When Jesus saw their faith, he said to the paralytic, "Son, your sins are forgiven." (Mark 2:3-5)

Key Concept: True friendship

Materials: Bible

One of my favorite stories from the New Testament is about the four friends who brought a paralyzed man to Jesus. Do you remember that story? *(Let the children respond. If they know portions of the story, let them share it with the group.)* This story is found in Mark 2:1-12. Many people heard that Jesus was home. They crowded into the house and no one else could enter. *(Open Bible.)* Mark 2:3-5 says, *Then some people came, bringing to him a paralyzed man, carried by four of them. And when they could not bring him to Jesus because of the crowd, they removed the roof above him; and after having dug through it, they let down the mat on which the paralytic lay. When Jesus saw their faith, he said to the paralytic, "Son, your sins are forgiven."* Some of the scribes couldn't believe that Jesus forgave the man's sins. Jesus then told the man to pick up his mat and walk. He did and everyone was amazed and praised God.

This paralyzed man had some very special friends. They could have given up after seeing all the people crowded around the door. They were determined to get their friend to Jesus and they did. It wasn't just the man's faith that made him well, but also the faith of his friends who knew that Jesus could help him. They were true and faithful friends.

These friends can teach us how to be true and faithful. Whether we're at church, at school, or at home, we need to be faithful friends, too. When a friend is sick, we might send a card or collect his or her homework assignments. If a friend is sad, we might sit and talk with them. Our faith in Jesus can help us be better friends to those around us. We must remember what

Jesus said and taught about loving our neighbors and treating others the way we want to be treated. Let's all try hard this week to be faithful friends.

Seventh Sunday after Epiphany

Title: A Big "YES!"

Scripture: 2 Corinthians 1:18-22

Key Verse: For in him every one of God's promises is a "Yes."
(2 Corinthians 1:20a)

Key Concept: God's promises are true.

Materials: Bible

Have you ever made any promises that you didn't keep? *(Let the children respond.)* Probably one of the hardest promises to keep is not to tell a secret. It can be so hard to know something other people don't know. There are other times when we don't do what we say we were going to do. Have you told a friend you would do something and then didn't do it? *(Give the children a chance to respond.)* Have you ever promised your parents that you would clean up your room and then didn't do it? *(Let children respond.)*

One of our Bible lessons for today speaks about promises. *(Open Bible.)* Second Corinthians 1:20 says, *For in him every one of God's promises is a "Yes."* Through Jesus' coming, God shows God's trustworthiness and faithfulness. This brings us hope. Even in times when we fail to keep our promises, we know that God always keeps God's promises. Can you think of some promises that God has given to us? *(Let the children respond. Some examples are eternal life, forgiveness, love, God's presence, etc. You may want to elaborate for understanding.)* God's promises are always a big "Yes!" Let's thank God for keeping God's promises.

Eighth Sunday after Epiphany

Title: *Endless Forgiveness*

Scripture: *Psalm 103:1-13, 22*

Key Verse: *. . . as far as the east is from the west, so far he removes our transgressions from us. (Psalm 103:12)*

Key Concept: *God's forgiveness*

Materials: *Bible, marked map of the world or globe*

Preparation: *Mark the world map or globe at the place farthest east from your church and estimate the mileage to this place.*

Has anyone ever done something to hurt you and then asked for forgiveness or said I'm sorry? (*Let the children respond.*) Was it hard to forgive them? (*Let the children respond.*) Sometimes it's hard to forgive others for doing wrong to us. Sometimes we may still be upset with a person and even though we say we've forgiven them, we don't forget the wrong they did. God's forgiveness is different.

God's love for us is shown in so many ways, especially God's forgiveness of the things we do wrong. (*Open Bible.*) Psalm 103:12 says, *. . . as far as the east is from the west, so far he removes our transgressions from us. Transgressions* is another word for sin or the wrong things we do that don't follow God's way. Look at this map. I have marked the farthest place east from where we live. It's (blank) miles. That's a long way. In Bible times when this psalm was written, they didn't know how far east or west they could go. They just knew it was a long, long way. The writer of the psalm used this word picture of east and west to tell us that when God forgives, God forgets. God doesn't stay upset with us because we did something wrong. When we ask for forgiveness, we're forgiven and our sin is forgotten.

Eighth Sunday after Epiphany

Title: Following Jesus

Scripture: Mark 2:13-22

Key Verse: As he was walking along, he saw Levi son of Alphaeus sitting at the tax booth, and he said to him, "Follow me." And he got up and followed him. (Mark 2:14)

Key Concept: Discipleship

Materials: Bible

We're going to play a short game of "Follow the Leader." I'll be the leader and you do whatever I do. *(Try any motions that you feel comfortable doing. For the last motion, get up and tell the children to follow you. Walk out of the sanctuary into the foyer and then return to the front. As you lead the children through the congregation, stop and say to various adults, "follow me." Adults may or may not follow. Either way is fine.)*

That was an interesting game of "Follow the Leader." We even asked some of the adults to join us by saying, "Follow me." In our Scripture lesson today, Jesus calls one of his disciples to follow him. *(Open Bible.)* Mark 2:14 says, *As he was walking along, he saw Levi son of Alphaeus sitting at the tax booth, and he said to him, "Follow me." And he got up and followed him.* Levi left his job and followed Jesus. Jesus wants us to follow him, too. In our game, you followed me. In our lives, we need to follow Jesus every day and do the things that Jesus wants us to do. What are some things we can do or say that would show others we follow Jesus? *(Let the children respond. Affirm their answers by repeating them.)* There are many ways we can show that we follow Jesus. Let's all try very hard to follow Jesus in all that we do and say.

Transfiguration Sunday

Title: Listen!

Scripture: Mark 9:2-9

Key Verse: Then a cloud overshadowed them, and from the cloud came a voice, "This is my Son, the Beloved; listen to him!" (Mark 9:7)

Key Concepts: Jesus' transfiguration, listening and change

Materials: Bible

Sometimes it's hard to understand some of the things that happen in the Bible. Can you think of Bible stories where it's hard to understand why certain things happen? *(Let the children respond. If necessary, name familiar stories such as the parting of the Red Sea for the Israelites or Jonah living in a large fish for three days, etc.)* Today is called Transfiguration Sunday. Our story from the Gospel of Mark tells us about the transfiguration of Jesus. This is one of those stories that can be hard to understand or even imagine.

Jesus took Peter, James, and John and went up on a mountain. Right before the disciples' eyes, Jesus was transfigured. This means that Jesus changed. Jesus shone with heavenly glory and he talked with Moses and Elijah. How do you think Peter, James, and John felt when they saw this? *(Let the children respond.)* The Bible says that they were terrified. It really scared them. But then something amazing happened. *(Open Bible.)* Mark 9:7 says, *Then a cloud overshadowed them and from the cloud came a voice, "This is my Son, the Beloved; listen to him!"* It was important for the disciples to know that Jesus was special. Jesus was God's Son and had a lot to teach the disciples about God's kingdom. The disciples were told to listen to Jesus. I'm sure this changed how the disciples felt about Jesus.

We need to listen to Jesus, too. We know that Jesus is special, and we should learn how Jesus wants us to live. By listening and learning, we can be changed into the people Jesus wants us to be. Let's listen to Jesus.

Transfiguration Sunday

Title: Distractions

Scripture: 2 Corinthians 4:3-6

Key Verse: *In their case the god of this world has blinded the minds of the unbelievers, to keep them from seeing the light of the gospel of the glory of Christ, who is the image of God. (2 Corinthians 4:4)*

Key Concepts: Temptation and distractions

Materials: Bible

Preparation: Ask another adult to make a distraction during your time with the children.

I'm so glad you are here today. *(Let this be the cue for the other adult to begin distracting the children. The person may make faces or ask questions to get the children's attention away from you. At first, ignore the distraction and the children's reaction and continue your conversation.)* We can sing songs, pray, and listen as we worship God. Why are you all laughing? What's going on? *(Let the children explain what is happening.)*

I asked (the name of the person who is distracting) to get your attention away from me during our time together. It's easy to get distracted, isn't it? It's easy to let one thing take our attention away from something more important. This can also happen as we try to follow Christ. *(Open Bible.)* In 2 Corinthians 4:4, Paul wrote, *In their case the god of this world has blinded the minds of the unbelievers, to keep them from seeing the light of the gospel of the glory of Christ, who is the image of God.* People who don't believe in God have a hard time seeing or understanding the good news of Jesus. They are distracted by other things such as money, popularity, and possessions. If we aren't careful, we can be distracted from following Jesus, too. It's important for us to not give in to temptations and distractions. We should always ask ourselves if what we're doing or saying is pleasing to Jesus.

Common Lectionary
Year C

First Sunday of Advent

Title: A Waiting Prayer

Scripture: Psalm 25:1-10

Key Verses: Make me to know your ways, O Lord; teach me your paths. Lead me in your truth, and teach me, for you are the God of my salvation; for you I wait all day long. (Psalm 25:4-5)

Materials: Bible, Advent wreath, a copy of the key verses for each child

Preparation: Make a copy of the key verses for each child.

I would like for you to join me around the Advent wreath. Today is the first Sunday of Advent. We will light the first candle. after today, there are only three more Sundays before we celebrate Jesus' birth. *(Light or have one of the children light the first candle. Then have the children sit near the Advent wreath. Always use caution around fire.)*

Lighting these candles lets us see how long we have to wait for Christmas. What are some things that you have to wait for? (*Let the children answer. If needed, you might suggest birthdays, opening presents, waiting in line for your turn, etc.*) We wait for many things, and we know that they'll happen. The psalmist knew this, too. *(Open Bible.)* Psalm 25 is a song that is also a prayer. The person who wrote the psalm prayed, *Make me know your ways, O LORD; teach me your paths. Lead me in your truth, and teach me, for you are the God of my salvation; for you I wait all day long.* The psalmist trusted God and asked God to help him/her to follow God's ways. This person trusted God. This person was willing to wait all day long for God to work because God was faithful.

As we wait and count the days until Jesus' birth, we may want to pray the psalmist's prayer. Here is a copy of the verses we read together for you to put on your refrigerator. From now until Christmas, pray these verses with your family as a way to prepare for Jesus' coming. Make prayer an important part of getting ready for Jesus' birthday. Through prayer, God can help us know God's ways.

First Sunday of Advent

Title: Hearts of Holiness

Scripture: 1 Thessalonians 3:9-13

Key Verse: And may he so strengthen your hearts in holiness that you may be blameless before our God and Father at the coming of our Lord Jesus with all his saints. (1 Thessalonians 3:13)

Key Concept: Holiness

Materials: Bible, large red heart, marker

Have you ever thought about what it means to be "holy"? We hear this word in the hymns we sing and in Scripture readings. In our lesson today, we find a form of the word holy—"holiness." *(Open Bible.)* First Thessalonians 3:13 says, *And may he so strengthen your hearts in holiness that you may be blameless before our God and Father at the coming of our Lord Jesus with all his saints.* I brought this large red heart. We will write on the heart words that describe what holy/holiness means. What do you think it means? *(Let the children respond. Write on the heart answers that express the meaning. Suggest answers if needed: pure, perfect, loving, goodness, righteousness, etc.)* Holiness, like love, is hard to put into words that completely describe it.

Now that we have an idea of what it means to be holy, why is this so important as we begin the season of Advent? Advent is a time of preparing ourselves for Jesus' coming. The verse we read is part of a prayer that asks God to make God's people loving and holy. Only God can make us holy. We can't do it on our own. We need God's help and we know that we'll never be perfect. But as we prepare for Jesus' birth and coming, we can ask God to help us be loving and good like God is loving and good. We can ask God to make us pure so we can be ready for Jesus' coming.

Second Sunday of Advent

Title: The Promise Keeper

Scripture: Luke 1:68-79

Key Verse: "Blessed be the Lord God of Israel, for he has looked favorably on his people and redeemed them." (Luke 1:68)

Key Concept: God's faithfulness

Materials: Bible

Have you ever thought about Christmas as the celebration of a promise kept by God? (*Let the children respond.*) Sometimes as we're preparing for Christmas, we forget what it really meant for Jesus to come. If we think back to Old Testament times, God's promise and covenant began with Abraham. Throughout the Old Testament, we have stories of how God's people followed God. Then they would turn away and not follow God. God was always loving and forgiving and never left God's chosen people.

(*Open Bible.*) In Luke 1:68 Zechariah, the father of John the Baptist, spoke this prophecy: *Blessed be the Lord God of Israel, for he has looked favorably on his people and redeemed them.* Zechariah knew that God hadn't forgotten God's people. God was going to redeem them, which means to get them back. God sent Jesus to get God's people back.

So we can celebrate God's promise, too, because Jesus is our Savior, the one who brings us to God. What a wonderful promise keeper God is. When we say God keeps God's promise, we're saying that God is faithful. As we prepare for Jesus' birth, let's praise and thank God for keeping God's promise.

Second Sunday of Advent

Title: Sharing Good News

Scripture: Philippians 1:3-11

Key Verses: I thank my God every time I remember you, constantly praying with joy in every one of my prayers for all of you, because of your sharing in the gospel from the first day until now. (Philippians 1:3-5)

Key Concept: Sharing the good news

Materials: Bible

Let's start our time together by sharing any good news we have. Does anyone have good news—something that happened this week that made you happy or excited? *(Let the children raise their hands and share their good news. If you don't have volunteers, think of good news you can share and share it with excitement.)* When we have good news to share, it's easy to get excited. Whether we were invited to a fun party or received a brand-new pair of shoes, we get excited and we like to tell our friends all about it.

In Philippians, Paul wrote about how excited he was that the church was sharing the good news of Jesus. *(Open Bible.)* He wrote in Philippians 1:3-5, *I thank my God every time I remember you, constantly praying with joy in every one of my prayers for all of you, because of your sharing in the gospel from the first day until now.* Paul was joyful and excited that the church would continue to share the good news of Jesus.

As we prepare for Jesus' coming, we should also find ourselves filled with excitement about the good news of Jesus. This is a time when we can share with our friends the true meaning of Christmas. It's the birth of Jesus, our Savior and friend. Let's get excited about this good news and tell everyone that Jesus is coming!

Third Sunday of Advent

Title: Joy!

Scripture: Zephaniah 3:14-20

**Key Verses: Rejoice and exult with all your heart, . . . The king of Israel, the
Lord, is in your midst . . . . (Zephaniah 3:14b, 15b)**

Key Concept: Joy

Materials: Bible

Preparation: Prepare to sing the first verse of "Joy to the World."

We're getting closer to Christmas, and I'm sure you're all getting excited.
What are some things that excite you about this time of year? *(Let the children respond. Expect various answers and move on when they begin to repeat.)*
All these things we mentioned bring excitement because we've hoped for
them. Now they will soon happen.

That's how God's people felt when they heard the hopeful words of
Zephaniah. God's people hadn't been faithful and were sent away from their
home into what we call exile. Zephaniah gave them a word of hope that
brought them joy and excitement. *(Open Bible.)* Zephaniah 3:14b, 15b say,
*Rejoice and exult with all your heart, . . . The king of Israel, the LORD, is in your
midst . . . .* God hadn't forgotten God's people and their hopes to return
home. They would soon return to God. This brought them great joy. It
made them happy.

As we get closer and closer to the coming of Jesus, we have a reason to be
full of joy. Jesus is coming to be our Savior. One way we can express our
excitement and joy is to sing. I want us all to sing together the first verse of
"Joy to the World." *(Invite the congregation to sing if you wish.)* But before we
sing the words, listen to them. *(Read the words of the first verse, commenting
on the meaning if you have younger children.)* Now let's sing with joy knowing
that Jesus is with us.

Third Sunday of Advent

Title: What Should We Do?

Scripture: Luke 3:7-18

Key Verses: And the crowds asked him, "What then should we do?" In reply he said to them, "Whoever has two coats must share with anyone who has none; and whoever has food must do likewise." (Luke 3:10-11)

Key Concepts: Sharing, giving

Materials: Bible

Preparation: Present this sermon in connection with a food collection for the needy. Remind parents and children ahead of time to bring nonperishable food items for the collection.

(Invite the children bring their nonperishable food items to the front. Place the items around the altar, nativity scene, or another designated spot.) What should we do with the food items you brought this morning? *(Let the children respond. Be prepared for a variety of answers. Guide the discussion toward sharing/giving.)* The food we collect this morning will help people who don't have enough food to eat. Did you know there are many people who don't have enough food to eat each day? That makes me sad, but when I give food to someone who needs it, I feel happy to know that I can help. By bringing your food items, you're helping others by sharing what you have. You are giving the food to others who need help.

In Bible times, God's people waited for God to send them a Messiah, someone to save them. John the Baptist told these people that Jesus was coming. *(Open Bible.)* Luke 3:10-11 says, *And the crowds asked him, "What then should we do?" In reply he said to them, "Whoever has two coats must share with anyone who has none; and whoever has food must do likewise."*

John the Baptist told the crowd that to prepare for Jesus' coming, they needed to share what they had with others in need. Sometimes we need a reminder that Christmas is a time of giving, especially to those in need. But it shouldn't stop once the season is over. We all need to ask ourselves each day, "What should I do to prepare for Jesus?" Our answer should include sharing what we have with others in need.

Fourth Sunday of Advent

Title: Why Bethlehem?

Scripture: Micah 5:2-5a

Key Verse: But you, O Bethlehem of Ephrathah, who are one of the little clans of Judah, from you shall come forth for me one who is to rule in Israel, whose origin is from of old, from ancient days. (Micah 5:2)

Key Concept: Prophecy

Materials: Bible, map of Bible lands showing Bethlehem

Preparation: Prepare to sing "O Little Town of Bethlehem."

This is the last Sunday before Christmas. We've made preparations and we're ready for Jesus to come. Who can tell me where Jesus was born? *(Let the children answer.)* Let's look at this map and find Bethlehem. *(Find Bethlehem.)* Bethlehem is not a big place. It's a small town outside of Jerusalem. Jesus was to be the King and Savior of his people, yet he was born in this little village. Why do you think Jesus was born in Bethlehem? *(Let the children answer.)*

Long before Jesus came, God's people looked for a new king, someone who would save them from their enemies. *(Open Bible.)* The prophet Micah spoke these words: *But you, O Bethlehem of Ephrathah, who are one of the little clans of Judah, from you shall come forth for me one who is to rule in Israel, whose origin is from of old, from ancient days.* Most people probably think that a king would come from an important place and that everyone would know of his birth. Jesus' birth wasn't like that. The new king wasn't going to be born in the city, but in Bethlehem. He was born in a stable in Bethlehem with only a few people knowing the importance of what happened that night. When the New Testament was written, people saw the prophecy we read come true at the birth of Jesus.

The writer of the hymn "O Little Town of Bethlehem" recognized this prophecy and put it into poetry we can sing. Let's join together and sing the first verse of "O Little Town of Bethlehem."

Fourth Sunday of Advent

Title: I Believe!

Scripture: Luke 1:39-45

Key Verse: "And blessed is she who believed that there would be a fulfillment of what was spoken to her by the Lord." (Luke 1:45)

Key Concept: Trusting God's Word

Materials: Bible, tabloid newspaper with something unbelievable

I know some of you have seen these newspapers with big headlines about something unbelievable. They are placed on stands at the grocery store where you can't miss them. I brought one today and the headlines on it say [read an appropriate headline]. *(You may want to comment on how silly or ridiculous the title is.)* Most of these papers stretch the truth to get people to buy their newspaper. If you want to find out what is happening in the world, this isn't a trustworthy way to get correct information. Trustworthy means that something is true. Have you ever heard someone say, "Don't believe everything you hear or read"? We must think about who is giving the information and learn how trustworthy they are before we believe what they say.

Mary had to decide whether to believe what the angel Gabriel told her. The angel told her she would have a son and she was to name him Jesus. The angel said Jesus would be the Son of God. Mary wasn't even married yet, and she was going to have a baby. People would talk about Mary and her problem. But Mary chose to believe God's Word that came to her through the angel. *(Open Bible.)* In Luke 1:45 Elizabeth says to Mary, *"And blessed is she who believed that there would be a fulfillment of what was spoken to her by the Lord."* Mary believed and trusted God's Word. She is an example for us. As God's followers, we're no different from Mary. Like Mary, we must trust God's Word and say "I believe," even when some things seem impossible.

First Sunday after Christmas

Title: Who's Lost?

Scripture: Luke 2:41-52

Key Verse: But they did not understand what he said to them. (Luke 2:50)

Key Concepts: Jesus' childhood, trust

Materials: Bible

Preparation: Ask an adult to play the role of Mary and recite the monologue below.

Today is the first Sunday after Christmas. Our Bible lessons still focus on Jesus as a child. The story for today is about Jesus and his family going to Jerusalem for Passover when he was twelve. I have invited a guest from Bible times to tell you about this trip. Mary, come and tell the children about your Passover trip with Joseph and Jesus.

Mary's Monologue

Hi, children. When Jesus was twelve, something scary happened during our trip to Jerusalem. Everything was fine until we were ready to return home. Joseph thought Jesus was with some of our friends and family, so we didn't worry until a day or two went by. We asked people if they had seen Jesus. No one remembered seeing him. I grew very frightened. I had lost my child. How could I have let anything happen to him?

Joseph and I went back to Jerusalem to see if he was still there. We went to all the places we had visited during the Passover. The last place we looked was the temple. We walked in and found Jesus talking with the teachers of the temple. I didn't know whether to be angry or to hug him. When I asked him about his behavior, he said he was in his Father's house. He came home with us and obeyed us. I always wondered about that trip and what Jesus said. I didn't understand everything he told us. *(Exit.)*

How do you think Mary and Joseph felt when they found Jesus in the temple? *(Let the children respond.)* Why do you think Jesus stayed at the temple? *(Let the children respond. Open Bible.)* Luke 2:50 says, *But they did not understand what he said to them.* Mary and Joseph didn't understand everything Jesus did. They knew he was special, but they had to wait to see how this child from God would lead God's people. They had to trust God. Mary and Joseph thought Jesus was lost, but they learned that he was where he needed to be. They couldn't understand Jesus, but they trusted God anyway.

We have to trust Jesus to lead us. We don't always understand why something happens or what we need to do. But if we're obedient and seeking Jesus every day, Jesus will help us make the right choices. We have to trust and have the desire to love Jesus, even when we don't understand.

First Sunday after Christmas

Title: Be Like Jesus

Scripture: Colossians 3:12-17

Key Verse: And whatever you do, in word or deed, do everything in the name of the Lord Jesus, giving thanks to God the Father through him. (Colossians 3:17)

Materials: Bible, paper dolls

Preparation: Make simple paper dolls and print one of these words on each doll: compassion, kindness, humility, meekness, patience, forgiveness, love, peace, thankfulness.

Did you know that what we say or do lets other people know what kind of people we are? If I always tried to get my way, others might think I was selfish or bossy. If I always said mean things to people, others would think I was a bully. These are examples of what God doesn't want us to be. God doesn't want us to be selfish and mean. God wants us to be like Jesus. When we act like Jesus, we can let other people know that we're Jesus' followers.

In his letter to the Colossians, Paul gives us ways we should act to show we're God's chosen people. I wrote the words for these ways on paper dolls. *(Name each doll. Customize this portion for your group. Knowing the age and maturity of your group will make a difference in how you explain the attitudes.)*

It may seem impossible, but with God's help we can try to do and be all these things. *(Open Bible.)* Colossians 3:17 says, *And whatever you do, in word or deed, do everything in the name of the Lord Jesus, giving thanks to God the Father through him.* As we get up each morning, we should remind ourselves that we belong to God. We are thankful for what God has done for us, and we show our love for God by acting like Jesus. Then others will know we belong to Jesus.

First Sunday after Epiphany

Title: Say Glory!

Scripture: Psalm 29

Key Verse: . . . and in his temple all say, "Glory!" (Psalm 29:9b)

Key Concept: God's kingdom/reign

Materials: Bible, psalm litany (optional)

Preparation: (Optional) Prepare a litany based on the psalm. Have the words printed in the bulletin. Give the children a simple part, such as repeating "Glory!" after each set of phrases the congregation recites.

In worship, we often talk about God's kingdom and reign through our songs, prayers, and preaching. *(Give examples such as the Lord's prayer, hymns of praise, etc.)* Have you ever wondered what or where God's kingdom is? Each of us is a part of God's kingdom. God's kingdom is in all the earth. God has given us a beautiful world with trees, flowers, and animals of all kinds. I have a question for you. How do we care for the world that God has given us? You can name things we do well and things that we don't do well. *(Let the children respond.)*

God wants us to live in God's kingdom. That means caring for the earth and caring for each other. Sometimes we forget that the earth and each one of us belong to God. Out of our selfishness, we've harmed the earth and each other. Psalm 29 reminds us of God's kingdom, power, and glory. *(Open Bible.)* Our response to God should be like that of the psalm writer, who wrote, . . . *and in his temple all say, "Glory!"*

We see that we belong to God and we're to praise God's name. *(At this point you can either end the sermon or use one of the following options: 1. Read the entire Psalm 29 and have the children say the word "glory" when you point to them; or 2. Have the children and congregation participate in a litany based on the psalm.)*

We also celebrate Jesus' baptism today. When people are baptized, it shows that they belong to God. We can all say "Glory!"

First Sunday after Epiphany

Title: Just One

Scripture: Acts 8:14-17

Key Verse: Now when the apostles at Jerusalem heard that Samaria had accepted the word of God, they sent Peter and John to them. (Acts 8:14)

Key Concepts: Inclusiveness, one Church, one people of God

Materials: Bible

Have any of you ever been left out of something you really wanted to do—like a game or a party? *(Let the children respond.)* How does it feel to be left out? *(Let the children respond.)* It makes us feel that we don't belong and that we aren't important. Sometimes larger groups of people get left out. Some may get left out because of their skin color. Others may get left out because they don't have much money or power. There are lots of ways people get excluded or left out, but that's not God's way.

In Bible times, when the church was just beginning, most of the Christians were Jewish Christians. They were Jews who came to believe in Jesus as God's Son. Their church was in Jerusalem. But then the good news of Jesus began to spread. *(Open Bible.)* Acts 8:14 says, *Now when the apostles at Jerusalem heard that Samaria had accepted the word of God, they sent Peter and John to them.*

Samaritans and Jews usually didn't like each other. In fact, Jews would walk all the way around the country of Samaria when they traveled. They didn't want to meet any Samaritans on their journey, even though it would be faster to walk straight through the country. This makes the story exciting because Jewish Christians were telling Samaritans about Jesus. They had changed their minds about the Samaritans and wanted to share the good news with them. These Samaritans were baptized in the name of Jesus. Peter and John laid hands on them and they received the Holy Spirit.

The Jewish Christians and the apostles in Jerusalem recognized that the one God whom they loved was the same God who loved the Samaritans. God didn't love one group more than another. God sent Jesus so that everyone who believes can be a part of the one people of God, with one baptism, one Church, and one Spirit. God includes everybody, and we can celebrate that we're part of one people of God.

Second Sunday after Epiphany

Title: *Mysterious Generosity*

Scripture: *John 2:1-11*

Key Verse: *Jesus did this, the first of his signs, in Cana of Galilee, and revealed his glory; and his disciples believed in him. (John 2:11)*

Key Concepts: *God's mystery and generosity*

Materials: *Bible*

Our Scripture lesson for today is the story of Jesus at a wedding. Jesus, his disciples, and his mother Mary were invited to a wedding. The bride and groom must have expected only a small number of guests because they ran out of wine. Mary told Jesus about the wine. Jesus replied that it wasn't their place to fix the problem. But Mary told the servants nearby to do what Jesus said. Jesus told the servants to take six water jars and fill them to the top. Each of these jars held 20-30 gallons of water. Then Jesus told them to take some of the water to the head waiter for the party. The servants did as Jesus had said. The head waiter was surprised because the wine tasted very good. The good wine was normally served first, but this time the good wine came last. *(Open Bible.)* John 2:11 says, *Jesus did this, the first of his signs, in Cana of Galilee, and revealed his glory; and his disciples believed in him.*

This is an interesting story about Jesus. Even people who study the Bible as their job have a hard time understanding this story. First, Jesus says he and Mary shouldn't be concerned with the situation. A short time later, Jesus tells the servants to fill the water jugs. Then Jesus works his first miracle, changing the water to wine. Why do you think Jesus did this miracle? *(Let the children respond. Remind them that there are no wrong answers.)*

Most of the stories we read about Jesus show him meeting people's specific needs. He heals the sick and gives food to those who are hungry. In this story, at first Jesus doesn't seem to want to help, but then he turns 120 to 180 gallons of water into wine. That's a lot of wine! We can see how Jesus gives more than what we need. Jesus gives us more than we can even measure. The disciples believed when they saw Jesus' miracle. Do we believe in Jesus?

Second Sunday after Epiphany

Title: Teamwork

Scripture: 1 Corinthians 12:1-11

Key Verse: To each is given the manifestation [gifts] of the Spirit for the common good. (1 Corinthians 12:7)

Key Concept: We are to use our gifts for the good of the church.

Materials: Bible, baseball

Today I brought a baseball. I want everyone to sit around in a circle so we can roll the ball to each other. As we roll the ball, I want you to tell me one thing that makes a good baseball team. I'll start. A good baseball team has a good pitcher. *(Roll the ball to another child. Another option is simply to hand the ball from person to person.)*

We have said that a good baseball team has good pitchers, good hitters, people who can catch and throw in the field, etc. Even on the best baseball teams, a great pitcher may not be such a great hitter. The best fielders may not be the best pitchers. The fastest runners may not be such good catchers. On a good baseball team, each player works to be good at the position he or she holds. A good team has players who are good at different parts of the game. When the players come together, they work toward winning the game.

We're a team here at church. God made us and gave us different gifts and talents to help our church be the best it can be. Some people speak well, some sing and play instruments, some enjoy teaching, some listen well, and others are good at many more things important in the life and work of our church. *(Open Bible.)* First Corinthians 12:7 says, *To each is given the manifestation [gifts] of the Spirit for the common good.* This means that we should use the gifts God gave us to help the community.

God didn't make us all alike. What if everybody at our church sang well and that was all? We wouldn't do much besides sing. It takes all of us, including you, to use the gifts that we've been given to help our church be what God intended us to be. Let's join together and be a team that works together to proclaim Jesus Christ as Lord.

Third Sunday after Epiphany

Title: Stand Up!

Scripture: Nehemiah 8:1-3, 5-6, 8-10

Key Verse: And Ezra opened the book in the sight of all the people, for he was standing above all the people; and when he opened it, all the people stood up. (Nehemiah 8:5)

Key Concept: Reverence for God's Word

Materials: Bible

This morning I want us to play a game. If you believe what I say is true, please stand up. *(You may use the list included or create your own, including a mixture of true and false. Let the children respond after each statement. Have them sit again before you read the next statement.)* 1. The sky is blue. 2. My hair is black. 3. Jesus is our friend. 4. It's raining today. 5. The Bible is God's Word. Sometimes we talk about standing up for what we believe in. When we stand up for what we believe in, we feel strongly about it.

In today's Old Testament story, Ezra stands by the Water Gate. He is ready to read the book of the law to God's people. *(Open Bible.)* Nehemiah 8:5 says, *And Ezra opened the book in the sight of all the people, for he was standing above all the people; and when he opened it, all the people stood up.* When Ezra opened the Scripture, the people stood up to show they believed in God's word. They had reverence for God's word. *Reverence* is another word for respect or honor.

Have you ever wondered why we stand during some hymns, readings, and prayers? We stand to show our reverence for God. We stand to show our allegiance to Christ, which is our promise to follow Christ. By standing, we show that we strongly believe what we sing, hear, or pray. It's a way for us to honor and praise the one who came to be our Savior. Stand up for what you believe in—Jesus Christ our Lord and Savior.

Third Sunday after Epiphany

Title: How Sweet It Is

Scripture: Psalm 19

Key Verse: More to be desired are they than gold, even much fine gold; sweeter also than honey, and drippings of the honeycomb. (Psalm 19:10)

Key Concept: The joy of following God's Word

Materials: Bible, crackers or bread cubes, honey, wet wipes

Preparation: Alert parents ahead of time that children will taste honey and bread/crackers during this sermon. If there are allergies, you may want to consider a substitute or use the other sermon for this day.

Have you ever tasted honey? I brought some honey and bread for you to try. I want you to tell me how it tastes. *(Give each child a small piece of bread or a cracker with a little honey. You may want to cube the bread and put a drop of honey on it to taste.)* How does the honey taste? *(Let the children respond. Hopefully, someone will tell you it is sweet.)* The honey does taste sweet.

Sometimes when people write poetry, they describe something by comparing it to something else. The writer of Psalm 19 compared his/her love of the law given by God to gold and the sweetness of honey. *(Open Bible.)* Psalm 19:10 says, *More to be desired are they than gold, even much fine gold; sweeter also than honey, and drippings of the honeycomb.*

The psalmist found joy in following God's word. When we read God's word, we should listen carefully and with joy. Sometimes we may read it and say to ourselves, "That's something else I have to do or not do." But we shouldn't think of God's Word as a book of "dos and don'ts." We should want to please God. Because we love God, we should want to follow God's word with joy. Reading God's word is the only way we can know what pleases God. We should want to please God every day.

Fourth Sunday after Epiphany

Title: When I Grow Up

Scripture: Jeremiah 1:4-10

Key Verse: "Do not be afraid of them, for I am with you to deliver you, says the Lord." (Jeremiah 1:8)

Key Concept: God's call

Materials: Bible

Has anyone ever asked you to do something you thought you couldn't do? *(Let the children respond. You may want to have a back up example in case no one responds.)* Did they encourage you to try even though you were ready to give up? *(Let the children respond.)*

In Old Testament times, the prophet Jeremiah thought he couldn't do the job God had for him. Jeremiah thought he was too young to speak God's words to the people. But God kept telling Jeremiah to go and speak. *(Open Bible.)* In Jeremiah 1:8, God says to Jeremiah, *"Do not be afraid of them, for I am with you to deliver you, says the LORD."*

God told Jeremiah that God would always be with him. Jeremiah listened to God, even when he felt that the job was too big. Jeremiah put himself in God's presence, and God used him to be a great prophet to the nations and to God's people.

What do you want to be when you grow up? *(Let the children respond.)* Sometimes you may wonder about what you will be one day. You may even wonder about what God wants you to become. I believe God has hopes and desires for all of us. If we place ourselves in God's care and presence, God can help us know what to become. God's desire for us is known as God's call. No matter what job we have, if God is most important in our lives, we will show God's love and justice in whatever we do. We could be a firefighter, a butcher, a farmer, a chemist, or do any other job and work for the glory of God.

Fourth Sunday after Epiphany

Title: Love Acts

Scripture: 1 Corinthians 13

Key Verses: Love is patient; love is kind; love is not envious or boastful or arrogant or rude. It does not insist on its own way; it is not irritable or resentful; it does not rejoice in wrongdoing, but rejoices in the truth. It bears all things, believes all things, hopes all things, endures all things. (1 Corinthians 13:4-7)

Key Concepts: Love, God's love

Materials: Bible, prepared paper with words/phrases

Preparation: Write these words on 8-x-11 inch paper: patient, kind, envious, rude, selfish, rejoices, bears all, believes all, hopes all, endures all.

One of the most popular chapters of the Bible is 1 Corinthians 13. Many people call it "the love chapter" because it's about love. In fact, it's beautiful poetry. Sometimes we forget to think about why these words were written. Paul wrote this letter to the Corinthian church. The people of the church weren't treating each other in a loving way. Let's read part of the chapter and see what Paul says about love. *(Open Bible.) Love is patient; love is kind; love is not envious or boastful or arrogant or rude. It does not insist on its own way; it is not irritable or resentful; it does not rejoice in wrongdoing, but rejoices in the truth. It bears all things, believes all things, hopes all things, endures all things.*

In these verses, Paul lists practical actions that describe love. Let's talk about some of these actions. *(At this point, use your prepared paper to discuss some of the action words that describe love. Help children understand the meanings of the words. Do as many as your time allows.)*

As we talked about the different actions of love, did you see that love is important when we go through hard times? You don't have to be patient unless you are really waiting for something. You don't have to endure if everything is going well. Love helps us be unselfish because we're truly interested in the other person. Love can help us treat others in a kind way.

We need to remember God's love for us. God loves us even though we do things that aren't pleasing and loving to God. God can help us love when it's hard to love. This week, think about ways to show love as you're with friends and family. Ask God to help you love even when it's hard to do.

Fifth Sunday after Epiphany

Title: Who? Me?

Scripture: Isaiah 6:1-8 (9-13)

Key Verse: Then I heard the voice of the Lord saying, "Whom shall I send, and who will go for us?" And I said, "Here am I; send me!" (Isaiah 6:8)

Key Concepts: God's power, God's will

Materials: Bible

This morning I'd like some of you to help me. *(Ask a child you know well to do a task you know he or she will resist doing. You might ask a shy child to sing a solo of a song you pick, or ask a child to preach the sermon. Choose tasks that fit your context.)*

Most (all) of you refused to do what I asked you to do. I don't know all the reasons why you said no. You may have felt like you weren't ready, or maybe you were scared to do it.

Isaiah felt that way when God called him to be a prophet. He couldn't believe God would want him to bring God's words to others. He even says, "Woe is me!" Isaiah was scared and felt like he wasn't ready for the job, but God prepared him. God told him his sins were forgiven. *(Open Bible.)* This is recorded in Isaiah 6:8: *Then I heard the voice of the Lord saying, "Whom shall I send, and who will go for us?" And I said, "Here am I; send me!"* Isaiah knew God would help him. God wanted him to take a message to God's people. Isaiah had the desire and love for God to do what God wanted. Isaiah followed God's call.

How do we know what God wants us to do? *(Let the children answer. Expect various answers.)* If we follow God and love God, we will know and do what God wants us to do. You can be a nurse, a plumber, a computer programmer, or do any other job and still bring glory to God. It doesn't matter what job we have as long as God is always a part of the choices we make.

Fifth Sunday after Epiphany

Title: Fishing

Scripture: Luke 5:1-11

Key Verse: Then Jesus said to Simon, "Do not be afraid; from now on you will be catching people." (Luke 5:10b)

Key Concepts: Following Jesus, missions

Materials: Bible, prepared fish shapes, paper clips, small fishing pole or stick with fishing line attached, magnet

Preparation: Cut construction paper into simple fish shapes. Write the verses from Luke 5:1-11 on the fish shapes, one verse per fish. Number the fish. Write the key verse on additional fish if you expect more than eleven children. Attach paper clips to the fish shapes. Secure a magnet to the fishing line. Lay the fish shapes on the floor so the children can "catch" them with the fishing pole.

Do any of you like to go fishing? *(Let the children answer.)* Today, I've brought a fishing pole and fish to catch. *(Place the fish with verses 1-11 on the floor and tell everyone to pretend the floor is a pond. Include extra fish if needed. Give every child a chance to fish.)* Some fish have a number. Let's begin with number one and read the verses. *(Continue until all eleven verses are read. Assist nonreaders.)*

We have just read about a fishing story that took place in New Testament times. Many people worked as fishers to provide food for others. The fishermen in our story had been fishing all day, but they hadn't caught a single fish. They decided to let Jesus teach from one of their boats. Then Jesus told them to throw their nets into the water. When the fishermen pulled the nets from the water, they saw that the nets were full of fish! Jesus told the fishermen that they would catch people. What do you think he meant by that? *(Let the children respond.)*

Jesus was telling the fishermen to be his disciples and follow him. They left their jobs to go with Jesus. That's amazing to us. Jesus wants us to follow him and to "catch" people. As Jesus' followers, we're to tell others about Jesus. We're to be kind and gentle like Jesus and show others what Jesus is like. Think about ways that you can tell others about Jesus this week. It's important that we show the love of Jesus in all that we do and say. Let's go fishing!

Sixth Sunday after Epiphany

Title: True Happiness

Scripture: Jeremiah 17:5-10

Key Verse: Blessed are those who trust in the Lord, whose trust is the Lord. (Jeremiah 17:7)

Key Concept: Trusting God

Materials: Bible

This morning, I'd like to ask you a question. What makes you happy? *(Let the children respond. Expect a variety of answers. Affirm their answers by repeating them.)*

You have mentioned many things that make you happy. Some of you feel happy when you play with your toys or when you get presents. These things are fun, but they can break or you can outgrow them as you get older. One day, they won't be as much fun. They don't bring happiness that lasts a long time. *(Open Bible.)* In Jeremiah 17, we can find out how to have true happiness. Verse 7 says, *Blessed are those who trust in the LORD, whose trust is the LORD.* We call verses that begin with "Blessed are . . ." Beatitudes. You could replace the word "blessed" with "happy." Then the verse would say, *[Happy] are those who trust in the LORD.*

Sometimes the things people say bring happiness don't bring true happiness. Sometimes people want to feel happy in selfish ways: "If I just had this, I would be so happy." Jeremiah teaches us that true happiness isn't something you get. It's something that happens when we choose to trust God. When we trust God and follow God's way, we can be truly happy.

Sixth Sunday after Epiphany

Title: Expect the Unexpected

Scripture: Luke 6:17-26

Key Verses: Then he looked up at his disciples and said: "Blessed are you who are poor, for yours is the kingdom of God. Blessed are you who are hungry now, for you will be filled. Blessed are you who weep now, for you will laugh." (Luke 6:20-21)

Key Concept: God's wisdom

Materials: Bible, peeled hard-boiled egg (medium-sized), baby bottle, strip of paper, matches or lighter

Preparation: Decide whether this trick is appropriate for your place of worship. Practice the trick before the service.

Today I want to show you something neat. I'm going to make this whole egg fit into this bottle. *(Show the bottle and egg.)* Do you think I can do it? *(Answers may vary.)* Let's see if I can get it to work. *(Practice this trick several times before you do it for the children. Use a strip of paper that will fit in the bottle. Light the paper and drop it quickly in the bottle, then immediately place the egg on top of the bottle to seal it. Because of the pressure change, the egg should be sucked into the bottle.)* You wouldn't think this egg would fit, but it does. Sometimes things happen differently than we expect. *(This can be true if the trick doesn't work! Use this as an example if the trick fails.)*

(Open Bible.) In Luke 6:20-21, Jesus says something we might not expect. *Then he looked up at his disciples and said, "Blessed are you who are poor, for yours is the kingdom of God. Blessed are you who are hungry now, for you will be filled. Blessed are you who weep now, for you will laugh.* We may wonder how people who are poor, hungry, or weeping could be blessed (happy). What Jesus said is different from what we expect.

God's wisdom is sometimes like that. *(Open Bible.)* In fact, 1 Corinthians 1:25 says, *For God's foolishness is wiser than human wisdom, and God's weakness is stronger than human strength.* God's wisdom is so much greater than our own wisdom. Sometimes it's hard to understand. We can expect the unexpected with God. But isn't it nice to know that God loves us and cares for us no matter what? God can use us in unexpected ways if we choose to follow God.

Seventh Sunday after Epiphany

Title: Good or Bad—God Provides

Scripture: Genesis 45:3-11,15

Key Verse: "And now do not be distressed, or angry with yourselves, because you sold me here; for God sent me before you to preserve life." (Genesis 45:5)

Key Concept: God provides

Materials: Bible

Has anyone ever made you so mad that you didn't want to see or talk to them anymore? Raise your hand. Can someone share what happened without sharing the name of the person who made you mad? *(Choose a child to respond or share your own example.)* All of us have had times when someone made us mad or angry.

Have any of you heard of Joseph from the Old Testament? *(Briefly summarize Joseph's story—the coat, being sold by his brothers, in prison in Egypt, interpreting the king's dream, the famine, and becoming one of the rulers in Egypt.)* In our lesson, Joseph tells his brothers who he is. Joseph could have been very angry with his brothers for the way they treated him, but Joseph knew God's way. Joseph knew that God had provided for him and his family through all the sadness and hard times. *(Open Bible.)* In Genesis 45:5, Joseph tells his brothers, *"And now do not be distressed, or angry with yourselves, because you sold me here; for God sent me before you to preserve life."*

Even though bad things had happened between Joseph and his brothers, Joseph was forgiving as God is forgiving. He knew God provided for his family and for all the people of the land. Sometimes bad things happen and we don't know why. We may even think God had forgotten us. But we need to remember that God is our provider, the one who loves us. God cares about what happens to us and won't let us go.

Seventh Sunday after Epiphany

Title: The Golden Rule

Scripture: Luke 6:27-38

Key Verse: "Do to others as you would have them do to you." (Luke 6:31)

Key Concept: Relationships with others

Materials: Bible, stop sign

(Hold up a stop sign.) If you're driving down the road and see this sign, what are you supposed to do? *(Let the children respond.)* You're supposed to stop and look both ways before you go again. If you decided to not pay attention to the stop sign and kept on going, what do you think might happen? *(Let the children answer.)* Yes, you might have a wreck or you might be lucky that no other vehicle was coming. The stop sign is there for a reason. It's there for our safety. If we follow the rules of the road, we usually get where we want to go safely. Rules help us know how to be safe.

I'm sure you have rules at home and at school. We have rules so we can live and learn together peacefully. Rules help us show respect for each other. Our Scripture lesson has a verse that Jesus taught. It is an important rule. Some people call it the Golden Rule. *(Open Bible.)* Luke 6:31 says, *"Do to others as you would have them do to you."* Why do you think Jesus said this? *(Let the children respond.)* I think everyone wants to be treated in a kind and loving way. Jesus knew that. Sometimes we may not be kind or loving to a friend or family member. We need to ask ourselves if we want to be treated the way we're treating the other person. If the answer is "yes," then you're following Jesus' teaching. Let's try hard this week to follow the Golden Rule and show others that we respect and love them.

Eighth Sunday after Epiphany

Title: Plant the Word

Scripture: Isaiah 55:10-13

Key Verses: For as the rain and the snow come down from heaven, and do not return there until they have watered the earth, making it bring forth and sprout, giving seed to the sower and bread to the eater, so shall my word be that goes out from my mouth; it shall not return to me empty, but it shall accomplish that which I purpose, and succeed in the thing for which I sent it. (Isaiah 55:10-11)

Key Concept: God's Word

Materials: Bible, soil in a cup or pot, bean seeds, water, watering container

Today I brought gardening items. I have seeds, a container of water, and a pot with soil. Will someone volunteer to help? *(Call on two children to help— one to plant the seeds and one to water them.)* (Name) will plant the bean seeds I brought. (Name) will water our seeds. What else do our seeds need? *(Let the children answer.)* Once our seeds have had light, water, soil, and time, they'll grow into plants. The plants will produce beans that we can eat. Beans are good for us. They fill our tummies and nourish our bodies when we eat them.

In Bible times, people knew a lot about planting and growing their own food. They didn't have big supermarkets where they could get all the food they needed. They had to grow it themselves. In Scripture, the idea of planting food to nourish the body was sometimes used to explain something about God. Our Old Testament lesson uses the idea of planting seeds to talk about planting the word of God. You may wonder how you "plant" words of God. Listen to this passage. *(Open Bible.)* Isaiah 55:10-11 says, *For as the rain and the snow come down from heaven, and do not return there until they have watered the earth, making it bring forth and sprout, giving seed to the sower and bread to the eater, so shall my word be that goes out from my mouth; it shall not return to me empty, but it shall accomplish that which I purpose, and succeed in the thing for which I sent it.*

When we really listen to God's Word, it's like planting seeds. The seeds are words from God that change our lives. Words are planted in us when we listen to them. God's word nourishes us and fills us in a different way than food does. If the words we read from the Bible change us and we share them with others, we please and praise God with who we are. God's Word comes alive in us. Just like a plant that grows, we grow to become what God wants us to become.

Eighth Sunday after Epiphany

Title: What Have You Heard?

Scripture: Luke 6:39-49

*Key Verses: "Why do you call me 'Lord, Lord,' and do not do what I tell you?
I will show you what someone is like who comes to me, hears my
words, and acts on them. That one is like a man building a house, who
dug deeply and laid the foundation on rock; when a flood arose, the
river burst against that house but could not shake it, because it had
been well built." (Luke 6:46-48)*

Key Concept: Christian discipleship

Materials: Bible, picture of Jesus

Today I brought a Bible picture of the way someone thought Jesus
looked. I want us to think about the stories of Jesus we have heard. What do
those stories tell us about Jesus? I'll start. One of my favorite stories is how
Jesus loved children. Jesus thought children were important. What are stories
you know or what are words that describe Jesus? *(Let the children respond.)*

We know from reading and studying our Bibles at home and at church
that Jesus is a very special friend. One way we can show we want to follow
Jesus is to say Jesus is Lord. This means that Jesus is the one we want to
follow and serve. We want to be like Jesus. You have heard many stories
about Jesus and what he did while here on earth. Jesus came to teach us.
Jesus still teaches us as we hear the stories in the Bible. But we have to
remember that hearing the stories is not enough. We can know a lot about
Jesus, but to call Jesus Lord, we must do what we hear.

(Open Bible.) In Luke 6:46-48, Jesus said, *"Why do you call me 'Lord,
Lord,' and do not do what I tell you? I will show you what someone is like who
comes to me, hears my words, and acts on them. That one is like a man building
a house, who dug deeply and laid the foundation on rock; when a flood arose, the
river burst against that house but could not shake it, because it had been well
built."*

Calling Jesus Lord means we have to behave the way Jesus teaches. By
hearing and doing what Jesus teaches, we can know that we're well built.
We're Jesus' disciples, ready to serve.

Transfiguration Sunday

Title: Shining Faces

Scripture: 2 Corinthians 3:12–4:2

**Key Verse: . . . but when one turns to the Lord, the veil is removed.
(2 Corinthians 3:16)**

Key Concept: Following Jesus

Materials: Bible, veil

I need a volunteer today. I need someone to put on this veil I brought. *(Choose an older child who can answer the questions that follow.)* [Child's name], what can you see through the veil? *(Let the child answer.)* Can you see things clearly? *(Let the child answer.)* Now take off the veil. Can you describe the difference between seeing with the veil and seeing without the veil? *(Let the child respond and prompt if necessary.)*

In our Scripture lesson for today, Paul uses a veil to describe how Jesus brought a new way for all people to love and serve him. *(Open Bible.)* In 2 Corinthians 3:16, he wrote, *. . . but when one turns to the Lord, the veil is removed.*

Paul used the veil to remind us of an Old Testament story about Moses. Moses went up on the mountain and God spoke to him. When Moses came down to the people of Israel, his face shined and the people were afraid. Moses' face shined because he had been in the presence of God. To calm the people's fears, Moses placed a veil over his face. Moses told the people the rules that God wanted them to follow. Years later, Paul told a group of believers that the many laws were keeping them from following Jesus. They were so busy following the laws that they forgot about God. The laws blinded them to Jesus. They couldn't see. It was like they had a veil over their faces.

What are some of the things that keep us from following God? *(Let the children respond.)* When we choose to follow Jesus, everyone should be able to see that we belong to him. We should not hide behind a veil. Let your face shine for others to see the love of Jesus. In all you do or say, people will know if you belong to Jesus.

Transfiguration Sunday

Title: Awesome God

Scripture: Psalm 99

Key Verse: Extol the Lord our God, and worship at his holy mountain; for the Lord our God is holy. (Psalm 99:9)

Key Concepts: Praise, transfiguration

Materials: Bible

Today is Transfiguration Sunday. In our Gospel lesson, Jesus takes Peter, James, and John up a high mountain. Right before the disciples' eyes, Jesus is transfigured. *Transfigured* is a big word. It means changed. Jesus changed right before the disciples' eyes. He shined as he talked with Moses and Elijah. How do you think the disciples felt when they saw what happened to Jesus? *(Let the children respond.)* I think maybe they were scared and probably amazed. They saw something awesome! They would never be able to explain this in words. But they knew they had worshiped on the mountain. It was a holy place.

(Open Bible.) In Psalm 99, the psalmist sings praise to God for God's holiness. The psalmist writes, *Extol the LORD our God, and worship at his holy mountain; for the LORD our God is holy.* Sometimes the things God has done for us seem so big and unexplainable, yet we feel the need to praise God. What are some ways we can praise God? *(Let the children answer.)*

As we listen and pray today during worship, think about how awesome God is. Think about all that God has given you. Praise God with your whole self. To close, I want us to sing the "Doxology" as our prayer. *(Sing the "Doxology" and instruct the congregation to participate.)*

Appendix

Christmas I

Title: What's in a Name

Scripture: Isaiah 9:2-7

Key Verse: For a child has been born for us, a son given to us; authority rests upon his shoulders; and he is named Wonderful Counselor, Mighty God, Everlasting Father, Prince of Peace. (Isaiah 9:6)

Key Concept: Names that describe the nature of Jesus

Materials: Bible, baby name book with meanings

Today, we celebrate the birth of baby Jesus. When someone has a baby, one of the first things they do give the baby a name. When you were born, your parents picked a name for you. Some of you may have biblical names. Some of you may be named for other family members such as a grandmother or grandfather. Do any of you know why you were given your name? *(Choose two or three children to answer, then move on.)* Some parents name their children certain names because they like the sound or the meaning of the name. I brought a baby name book that has the meanings of names. Let's try a few of your names to see what they mean. *(Choose two or three children who don't normally participate and read the meanings of their names.)* Names describe who we are.

(Open Bible.) Isaiah 9:6 says, *For a child has been born for us, a son given to us; authority rests upon his shoulders; and he is named Wonderful Counselor, Mighty God, Everlasting Father, Prince of Peace.* In this verse we find names that describe the best king anyone could want. These are the names that we give to Jesus, because Jesus is the best king we could ever want. What do you think it means for Jesus to be called these names? *(Review each name in the verse, assisting with simple meanings when necessary.)*

These names describe who Jesus is. Jesus is one who brings power, might, love, care, peace, and prosperity. We can celebrate with joy today that Jesus is born. Jesus is the best king and Savior we could ever hope to have.

Christmas II

Title: Celebrating Jesus' Birth

Scripture: Luke 2:1-20

Key Verses: "I am bringing you good news of great joy for all people: to you is born this day in the city of David a Savior, who is the Messiah, the Lord." (Luke 2:10b-11)

Key Concept: Jesus' birth

Materials: Bible; Nativity scene with Mary, Joseph, baby Jesus, shepherds; small table

(Give the Nativity figures to some of the children. Guide them to arrange the figures on the table as you talk about each of the characters in the story. If the scene is already set, remove and hold each figure as you discuss the characters.) Today we celebrate the birth of baby Jesus. Luke tells us that Joseph and Mary traveled to Bethlehem because the government wanted to count all the people. Joseph's family was from Bethlehem, so they went to that town. While they were in Bethlehem, Mary had baby Jesus. He was born in a stable because there were no rooms left in town.

At the same time, shepherds were working in the field. It was their job to watch over the sheep. An angel appeared to them and announced the good news that the Savior was born in Bethlehem. The shepherds went to Bethlehem to see the child. They told Mary and Joseph what the angel had said. *(Open Bible.)* We can find the angel's words in Luke 2:10b-11: *"I am bringing you good news of great joy for all people; to you is born this day in the city of David a Savior, who is the Messiah, the Lord."*

(Show the Joseph figure.) How do you think Joseph felt knowing that this baby was so special? *(Children respond. Return Joseph figure to the table and show Mary figure.)* How do you think Mary felt about baby Jesus? *(Children respond. Return Mary figure to the table and show shepherd figure.)* How do you think the shepherds felt when the angel appeared to them gave them such good news? *(Children respond. Return shepherd figure to the table and show baby Jesus figure.)* How do you feel today knowing how special baby Jesus is? *(Let children respond and return baby Jesus figure to the table.)*

We can all celebrate with joy that Jesus has come to show us how to live and to give us eternal life. We can celebrate the love that comes to us at Christmas in baby Jesus.

Christmas III

Title: How Can We See

Scripture: John 1:1-14

Key Verse: The true light, which enlightens everyone, was coming into the world. (John 1:9)

Key Concept: Jesus' coming brings truth.

Materials: Bible, flashlight, light bulb, candle

What can you use to help you see in the dark? *(Let the children respond. Show the sources of light you brought.)* We have many ways to make light so we can see in the dark.

In the Bible, the writers sometimes use what we call symbols. A symbol is something that stands for something else. This can sometimes make the Bible hard to understand. One of the symbols in the Bible is light. We've talked about how we need light to see or find our way in the darkness. In the Gospel of John, the writer uses the word "light" to stand for Jesus. *(Open Bible.)* John 1:9 says, *The true light, which enlightens everyone, was coming into the world.* We could rewrite that verse to say Jesus came to earth to bring truth to everyone. Just as we need light to see when it is dark, we need Jesus to bring truth for our lives. This means Jesus can show us how to live in the world. Jesus can help us find our way each day to be the people he wants us to be.

We're all God's children, and we can celebrate the "light" that has come in Jesus. The light will help show us how to be God's children at home, at school, and at play.

Second Sunday after Christmas

Title: God's Generosity

Scripture: John 1:10-18

Key Verse: From his fullness we have all received, grace upon grace. (John 1:16)

Key Concept: Grace is God's generosity to us.

Materials: Bible, large bag of candy (enough for each child to have a handful)

Preparation: Ahead of time, enlist an adult or youth to help distribute candy at the end of the worship service.

Does anybody know what it means to be generous? *(Let children answer. Move ahead with the closest answers.)* A generous person freely and cheerfully gives what they have to others. I brought a bag full of candy today. How could I be generous with my candy? *(Let the children respond.)* To be generous, I would give each of you a handful of candy, wouldn't I? At the end of the worship service, you can come and get a handful of candy, with your parent's permission. [Name of enlisted adult or youth] will be here to help you.

God is generous to us. Can you name some things God has given to us freely and cheerfully? *(Let the children respond. Expect a variety of answers.)* God has given us the earth. We see the beautiful colors of trees in the fall, flowers in the spring, snow that blankets the earth in winter, green plants in the summer, animals, birds, and even insects. All of creation is so beautiful. God has given us all of this. God has also given us God's Son, Jesus. Jesus is God's most generous gift of all.

Have you ever heard the word "grace"? Some of our hymns use this word, and sometimes you hear me say it. Grace is God's generosity to us. *(Open Bible.)* John 1:16 says, *From his fullness we have all received, grace upon grace.* We could rewrite the verse to say that from God's fullness we have received generosity upon generosity. We can thank God for giving to us freely. We should ask God to help us be generous to others in need.

Second Sunday after Christmas

Title: Thanks for the Gifts

Scripture: Ephesians 1:3-14

Key Verse: . . . we, who were the first to set our hope on Christ, might live for the praise of his glory. (Ephesians 1:12)

Key Concept: God has chosen us and given us gifts of forgiveness, wisdom, and faith.

Materials: Bible

It has almost been two weeks since we celebrated Christmas. At Christmas, we give gifts and receive gifts from people we love. What's your favorite gift you received this year? *(Let each child respond. You may want them to raise their hands. Otherwise, go down the row until each child has shared.)*

In the book of Ephesians, we find the gifts God has given us in Jesus. One of the gifts is forgiveness. What does it mean to be forgiven? *(You can choose whether to let the children respond to this question.)* When we do something wrong that doesn't please God, we need to ask God for forgiveness. We also need to ask the person we have hurt for forgiveness. We call these wrong acts *sins*. God is so wonderful that God forgives and forgets our sins.

Another gift that God gives us is wisdom. As we seek to learn and live as God wants us to, God can help us know what pleases God. What are some ways we can learn how God wants us to live? *(Let the children respond.)* We can read our Bible, pray, study, listen in Sunday school, and participate in church activities such as missions and choir. In all these ways, God gives us wisdom as we seek to know God better.

The last gift I want us to talk about is God's gift of faith to us. God has chosen us and gives us the strength we need to believe. Sometimes it can be hard to believe in something you can't see or touch. But when we look at the special gift of Jesus, it's hard not to believe in a love so great. *(Open Bible.)* Because of these gifts and others we find in Ephesians 5:12, . . . *we, who were the first to set our hope on Christ, might live for the praise of his glory.* We show thanks for God's many gifts by living a life of praise and by following Jesus' example.

Epiphany Sunday

Title: The Shepherd King

Scripture: Matthew 2:1-12

*Key Verse: ". . . for from you shall come a ruler who is to shepherd my
people Israel." (Matthew 2:6b)*

Key Concept: Jesus as shepherd-king

Materials: Bible, crown

What do you think it would be like to be king or queen for a day? *(Show the
crown.)* I have a crown that I'm going let you wear. I want you to put it on
your head and tell me what you would do if you were king or queen. *(Give
the crown to each child in turn, letting children tell what they would do if they
were king or queen. After each child has a turn, review the characteristics of a
ruler that the children have given.)*

Today is Epiphany Sunday. We celebrate the wise men who followed the
star to find a new king. The wise men visited King Herod, who lived in
Jerusalem, and asked him where to find the child born to be King of the
Jews. King Herod was frightened. He didn't want to lose his power to rule
the people. When Herod asked the religious leaders where the Messiah was
to be born, they quoted an Old Testament prophet. They told Herod and
the wise men that the Messiah would be born in Bethlehem and that he
would be a shepherd-king. *(Open Bible.)* We find this Old Testament quote
in Matthew 2:6, . . . *for from you shall come a ruler who is to shepherd my
people Israel.*

Did you know that a shepherd is someone who guides, nurtures, protects, and cares for the sheep? This was a common job in Bible times. Jesus
was the new king who would rule like a shepherd. Jesus wasn't interested in
power and position. Jesus came to be a shepherd-king—one who loves, cares,
guides, and nurtures. We can ask Jesus to guide us and help us to love and
care for others like he cares for us.

Epiphany Sunday

Title: Now That We Know

Scripture: Ephesians 3:1-12

Key Verse: . . . *so that through the church the wisdom of God in its rich variety might now be made known to the rulers and authorities in the heavenly places. (Ephesians 3:10)*

Key Concept: *The revealing of Jesus calls the church to tell the good news and gives them strength for the task.*

Materials: Bible

Today is Epiphany Sunday. Do you know what "epiphany" means? It means to shine forth or to reveal something. If something is revealed, then you learn and know about something that you didn't know before. On Epiphany Sunday, we celebrate the wise men coming to Jesus by following the star. The star revealed something to them about Jesus—that Jesus was to be a special king.

What are some things you've learned about Jesus? *(Let the children answer. Expect a variety of answers. Affirm their answers by repeating them so the congregation can hear.)* At home and church, you've learned a lot about Jesus. We could say that what you've learned was revealed to you.

In Paul's letter to the Ephesians, Paul tells the church that because of the epiphany or revealing of Jesus, the church must tell the good news of Jesus. They would be given the strength to do that. *(Open Bible.)* In Ephesians 3:10, Paul writes, . . . *so that through the church the wisdom of God in its rich variety might now be made known to the rulers and authorities in the heavenly places.*

This verse teaches us about spreading the good news of Jesus to others. We talked about the different things we've learned about Jesus. Each of us is a part of the church, and we're to share the good news of Jesus with others. If we trust Jesus, he'll give us the strength and confidence we need to share the good news with the world.

Stewardship

Title: Our Offering

Scripture: 1 Chronicles 16:8-36

Key Verse: Ascribe to the Lord the glory due his name; bring an offering, and come before him. (1 Chronicles 16:29a)

Key Concept: Bringing our offering

Materials: Bible, prepared pie graph of church budget, offering envelope

Preparation: Using a pie plate or paper plate, prepare a simple pie graph that depicts how the church's money is spent. You might include home and foreign missions, church needs, building debts, salaries, etc.

(Hold up an offering envelope.) What do I have in my hand? *(Let the children respond.)* Why is it important that we bring our offering? *(Let the children respond. Expect a variety of answers. Affirm their answers by repeating them.)* Our offering is important for all of those reasons. I brought a simple pie graph to show you how our church spends money. When we put all our money together, we can do many things to help other people that we couldn't do alone. We can help others know and learn about God's love.

The most important reason we bring our offering is found in 1 Chronicles 16:29. *(Open Bible.)* It says, *Ascribe to the LORD the glory due his name; bring an offering, and come before him.*

The reason we bring our offering is to praise God and to show our thankfulness for all God has given us. Bringing our offering is an important part of worship. We should want to give cheerfully and generously. This is one way we show God our praise and thankfulness.

Stewardship

Title: Cheerful Giving

Scripture: 2 Corinthians 9:6-15

Key Verse: Each of you must give as you have made up your mind, not reluctantly or under compulsion, for God loves a cheerful giver. (2 Corinthians 9:7)

Key Concept: Giving willingly

Materials: Bible

I want to tell you a true story about giving. A children's Sunday school class led a church in a toy drive. The toys were to go to needy children in the area and around the world. The children's Sunday school teacher encouraged them to do odd jobs to earn money. Then they could buy toys to give with their own money. The teacher planned a trip for the class to go shopping and to eat at a restaurant together. The day arrived for the trip, but only one child came to go shopping. This child went with the teacher to buy toys for needy children. He had a wonderful time choosing toys for others. But he couldn't understand why his friends didn't want to go shopping. Why do you think his friends didn't want to go? *(Let the children respond.)* The child's teacher told him that you can't make other people do things they don't want to do.

(Open Bible.) Second Corinthians 9:7 says, *Each of you must give as you have made up your mind, not reluctantly or under compulsion, for God loves a cheerful giver.* Each of us is to give our money and our time to God willingly. Nobody should make us do it. We should want to do things for others out of our love for God. Each of us has to decide if we will give cheerfully to God. Will you?

Missions

Title: How Far Will It Go?

Scripture: Mark 16:9-18

Key Verse: And he said to them, "Go into all the world and proclaim the good news to the whole creation." (Mark 16:15)

Key Concept: Missions

Materials: Bible, globe

When we talk about missions, we often talk about giving our missions offering. We talk about telling others around the world the good news of Jesus. These are a part of doing missions. Do you ever feel that you're too young to do missions because you don't have much money and you can't travel around the world? I brought a globe today. We'll dream about where we'd like to go. First, let's find where we live on the globe. *(Turn the globe and find your location.)* Where are some places you would like to go if you could? *(Let the children respond. Find the places on the globe.)*

It would be neat to go to any of those places. We could share the good news there. But most of us aren't world travelers—at least not yet. Still, you can follow the teaching of Jesus from Mark 16:15. *(Open Bible.) And he said to them, "Go into all the world and proclaim the good news to the whole creation."*

Have you ever thought about this? When you share the good news with someone, they may share with another person. That person may share the good news with someone from another place. We never know how far the news we share about Jesus will go. That's why it's important for us to tell others the good news of Jesus right where we are. How far will the good news go?

Love

Title: Being Loving

Scripture: 1 John 4:7-21

Key Verse: Beloved, since God loved us so much, we also ought to love one another. (1 John 4:11)

Key Concept: Loving God and others

Materials: Bible, prepared hearts

Preparation: Cut heart shapes from pink or red construction paper. Print the key verse on each heart. Prepare enough hearts so that each child may have one.

What word do you think of when you see heart shapes? *(Let the children respond. Someone will say love.)* Why do we think of love when we see heart shapes? *(Let the children respond.)*

I want each of you to take one of these hearts. On this heart, you will find a Bible verse about love. If you can read, let's read it together. *Beloved, since God loved us so much, we also ought to love one another,* 1 John 4:11.

This verse tells us that God loved us. How do we know this? *(Let the children respond. Guide them to think about Jesus.)* God sent Jesus into the world so that our sins could be forgiven. God sent Jesus to teach us how to live. Love doesn't begin with us. It begins with God. If we know God, then we know love. The way we act and the words we say should show God's love to others.

Who are we to love? Can we choose who we love? *(Let the children respond.)* God wants us to love everyone. How can we show love to others? *(Let the children respond.)* How we treat people, how we spend our time, the choices we make, and being a true friend are all ways that we can show love to others. As you're with your friends and family this week, think about how you treat them. Think about what you say and what you do, and ask yourself if you're being loving like God is loving.

Family

Title: Honoring Parents

Scripture: Exodus 20:1-17

Key Verse: Honor your father and mother, so that your days may be long in the land that the Lord your God is giving you. (Exodus 20:12)

Key Concept: Family

Materials: Bible

This morning, I want us to talk about our families. *(Tell the children who makes up your family. For example, yourself, your husband, and your two children.)* Who is part of your family? *(Let the children take turns responding. Expect a variety of family types. Emphasize that families are all different.)* We have all different types of families, but all families are special and truly gifts from God.

(Open Bible.) Exodus 20:12 says, *Honor your father and mother, so that your days may be long in the land that the LORD your God is giving you.* This is one of the Ten Commandments given to Moses for God's people to follow. Why do you think God included honoring our fathers and mothers in the Ten Commandments? *(Let the children respond. Tell them there is no right or wrong answer.)*

Honoring our fathers and mothers is a way of showing respect and love to them. God has given us the gift of family. Some of you may have one parent, some two, some aunts or uncles, and some grandparents. Whoever makes up your family, God thought that mothers and fathers were important enough to be part of the ten rules God gave. We should honor, love, and respect those who are our parents. We also need to thank them for what they do for us.

Family

Title: Obedience

Scripture: Colossians 3:18-4:6

Key Verse: Children, obey your parents in everything, for this is your acceptable duty in the Lord. (Colossians 3:20)

Key Concept: Family

Materials: Bible

Preparation: Ahead of time, enlist an older female child to be the leader for the game "Mother, May I?" Tell her to allow only one particular child to move forward throughout the game.

I want us to play a game this morning. You may have played it before. It's called "Mother, May I?" I need [child's name] to be the leader. The rest of you will stand here in a line facing [child's name]. She will give each of you instructions. When she gives you an instruction, you must ask, "Mother, may I?" If she says, "Yes, you may," do what she has told you to do. If she says, "No, you may not," stay in your place. *(As one child is always allowed to move forward while the others never receive permission, complaining may arise. Stop the game accordingly.)*

Let's stop our game and talk a moment. How did you like the game? *(Let the children respond.)* I told [child's name] only to let one of you move during the game. It was hard to stand there and not get to move. It was hard to obey what [child's name] said, wasn't it? Sometimes it just doesn't seem fair. This happens in our families as well. Our parents ask us to do things and sometimes we don't like what we hear. We don't want to do what they ask. *(Open Bible.)* But in our Scripture lesson for today, Colossians 3:20 says, *Children, obey your parents in everything, for this is your acceptable duty in the Lord.* Paul wrote this letter to a church. He said obeying parents is a part of our Christian duty. It's a rule. We should obey our parents and honor them. That's what Jesus wants us to do out of our love for him and for our parents.

Friendship

Title: True Friends

Scripture: Proverbs 17:17

Key Verse: A friend loves at all times, and kinsfolk are born to share adversity. (Proverbs 17:17)

Key Concept: True friendship

Materials: Bible

As we are growing up, friends are important to us. Do you have a special friend with whom you like to spend time? *(Let the children respond.)* It is fun to play with friends, go to special events together, have them over to your house, and invite them to a party. There are many fun things we can do with our friends.

Have you ever thought about what a true friend is like when things aren't fun? For example, something embarrassing happens to you at school and some of the children tease you about it. Would a true friend do that? *(Let the children respond.)* What do you think a true friend is like? *(Let the children respond.)*

When I was growing up, I learned a song that I still remember. These are the words:

A friend loveth at all times when things are good or bad
A friend loveth at all times, rejoices when we're glad
A friend helpeth in trouble, a friend is always true
A friend loveth at all times, a friend I'll be to you.

(Open Bible.) This song is based on Proverbs 17:17, which says, *A friend loves at all times, and kinsfolk are born to share adversity.*

I want you to know that I'll be your friend when things are good or bad. I hope that you'll try to be a true friend to others in good and bad times. Sometimes it may be hard not to do what others do, like teasing someone else, but if we call that person our friend, we need to remember to love and not to tease. Teasing can hurt a person. God wants us to love our friends all the time.

Bibliography

The New Oxford Annotated Bible. New Revised Standard Version. Edited by Bruce M. Metzger and Roland E. Murphy. New York: Oxford University Press, 1991.

Texts for Preaching: A Lectionary Commentary Based on the NRSV—Year A. Edited by Walter Brueggemann et al. Louisville KY: Westminster John Knox Press, 1995.

Texts for Preaching: A Lectionary Commentary Based on the NRSV—Year B. Edited by Walter Brueggemann et al. Louisville KY: Westminster John Knox Press, 1993.

Texts for Preaching: A Lectionary Commentary Based on the NRSV—Year C. Edited by Charles B. Cousar et al. Louisville KY: Westminster John Knox Press, 1994.

Scripture Index

Old Testament Scripture Texts

Jeremiah 1:4-10	Fourth Sunday after Epiphany—C
Jeremiah 17:5-10	Sixth Sunday after Epiphany—C
Jonah 3:1-5, 10	Third Sunday after Epiphany—B
Micah 5:2-5a	Fourth Sunday of Advent—C
Micah 6:1-8	Fourth Sunday after Epiphany—A
Zephaniah 3:14-20	Third Sunday of Advent—C

New Testament Scripture Texts

Matthew 1:18-25	Fourth Sunday of Advent—A
Matthew 2:1-12	Epiphany—A, B, C
Matthew 3:1-12	Second Sunday of Advent—A
Matthew 4:12-23	Third Sunday after Epiphany—A
Matthew 5:1-12	Fourth Sunday after Epiphany—A
Matthew 5:13-20	Fifth Sunday after Epiphany—A
Matthew 5:38-48	Seventh Sunday after Epiphany—A
Matthew 6:24-34	Eighth Sunday after Epiphany—A
Matthew 17:1-9	Transfiguration Sunday—A
Mark 1:1-8	Second Sunday of Advent—B
Mark 1:4-11	First Sunday after Epiphany—B
Mark 1:40-45	Sixth Sunday after Epiphany—B
Mark 2:1-12	Seventh Sunday after Epiphany—B
Mark 2:13-22	Eighth Sunday after Epiphany—B
Mark 9:2-9	Transfiguration Sunday—B
Mark 13:24-37	First Sunday of Advent—B
Mark 16:9-18	Missions
Luke 1:26-38	Fourth Sunday of Advent—B
Luke 1:39-45	Fourth Sunday of Advent—C
Luke 1:47-55	Fourth Sunday of Advent—B
Luke 1:68-79	Second Sunday of Advent—C
Luke 2:1-20	Christmas II—A, B, C
Luke 2:22-40	First Sunday after Christmas—B
Luke 2:41-52	First Sunday after Christmas—C
Luke 3:7-18	Third Sunday of Advent—C
Luke 5:1-11	Fifth Sunday after Epiphany—C
Luke 6:17-26	Sixth Sunday after Epiphany—C
Luke 6:27-38	Seventh Sunday after Epiphany—C
Luke 6:39-49	Eighth Sunday after Epiphany—C
John 1:1-14	Christmas III—A, B, C

Subject Index

God's favor	First Sunday after Christmas—B
God's kingdom	Eighth Sunday after Epiphany—A
	First Sunday after Epiphany—C
God's love	Fourth Sunday after Epiphany—C
God's power	First Sunday after Epiphany—A
	Sixth Sunday after Epiphany—A
	Fourth Sunday of Advent—B
	First Sunday after Epiphany—B
God's presence	Third Sunday of Advent—A
	Third Sunday after Epiphany—A
	First Sunday of Advent—B
God's promises	Seventh Sunday after Epiphany—B
God's wisdom	Sixth Sunday after Epiphany—C
God's word	Third Sunday after Epiphany—C
	Eighth Sunday after Epiphany—C
Grace	Second Sunday after Christmas—A, B, C
Holiness	First Sunday of Advent—C
Hope	First Sunday of Advent—B
	Third Sunday of Advent—B
Jesus' birth	Christmas II—A, B, C
Jesus' identity	Fourth Sunday of Advent—A
	First Sunday after Epiphany—B
	Christmas I—A, B, C
	Epiphany—A, B, C
Joy	Third Sunday of Advent—C
Justice	Fourth Sunday after Epiphany—A
Listening	Second Sunday after Epiphany—B
	Transfiguration Sunday—B
Love for others	Fourth Sunday after Epiphany—B
	Seventh Sunday after Epiphany—C
	Appendix
Missions	Appendix
Mystery	Second Sunday after Epiphany—C
Peace	First Sunday of Advent—A
Praise	Transfiguration Sunday—C
Prayer	First Sunday of Advent—C
Prophets/Prophecy	Fourth Sunday after Epiphany—B
	Fourth Sunday of Advent—C
Sadness	Third Sunday of Advent—B
Telling others about Jesus/witness	Second Sunday of Advent—A
	Second Sunday after Epiphany—A
	Fifth Sunday after Epiphany—A
	Second Sunday of Advent—B
	Second Sunday of Advent—C
	Epiphany—A, B, C
Temptation	First Sunday after Christmas—A

SMYTH & HELWYS HELP! BOOKS

The Help series is an ongoing collection of guides designed as a resource for ministry leaders and lay people who face challenges within the church. Ranging from tips on preparing a children's sermon to caregiving directions in crisis situations, these books help churches become better equipped for the demands of ministry in today's world.

Crisis Ministry: A Handbook
Daniel G. Bagby

Covering more than 25 crisis pastoral-care situations, this book provides a practical guide for deacons, ministers, and other caregivers.

Drama Ministry: A Guidebook
Nancy Backues, Kerry Beaman, and Wendy Briggs

Drama Ministry: A Guidebook is a one-stop manual for starting, directing, and managing a drama ministry. Lay leaders who have no formal drama training to leaders who are experienced in drama will glean from the authors 25+ years of drama training and experience.

A Christian Educator's Book of Lists
Israel Galindo

This book is a reference manual of basic information that every Christian educator should have on hand. Part basic encyclopedia, part trivia resource, part practical "how to" compilations, part teaching manual, and part general knowledge index, this handbook provides "everything you need to know about Christian education but didn't know where to find."

Divorce Ministry: A Guidebook
Charles Qualls

This book shares with readers the value of establishing a divorce recovery ministry while also offering practical insights on establishing your own unique church-affiliated program. It provides helpful resources to guide you through the emotional and relational issues divorced people often encounter.

SMYTH&HELWYS.

Help! I'm Leading a Children's Sermon, Vol 1: Advent to Transfiguration Sunday
Marcia Taylor Thompson

This collection of over 70 ready-to-use sermons contains two children's sermons for each Sunday with an emphasis on Scripture, including key verses to be read within the sermon. The sermons invite children to participate in corporate worship in a meaningful, creative way by asking questions and using hands-on activities to explain themes such as hope, forgiveness, repentance, and God's sovereignty.

Help! I Teach Children's Sunday School
B. Max Price

This practical book is a must-read for both first-time and experienced teachers, with information on children from birth through sixth grade. Topics include: A Look at Today's Children, Characteristics of Effective Teachers, Teaching Different Age Groups, Teaching Special Needs Children, What about Discipline?, and much more.

Help! Our Church Is Growing: What to Do When the Old Ways No Longer Work
Mark Phillips

Phillips presents the story of a church in danger of being crushed under the weight of its own growth. This is a survival manual for those whose prayers have been answered.

Help! I'm Leading a Children's Sermon, Vol 2: Lent to Pentecost
Marcia Taylor Thompson

Following the Common Lectionary, there are two sermons for each Sunday with an appendix that contains sermons for Sundays where the Scripture is the same for all three years. The sermons are conversational in nature and focus on Scripture as the source of proclamation.

Help! I Teach Youth Sunday School
Brian Foreman, Bo Prosser, & David Woody

Real-life stories are mingled with information on Youth and their culture, common myths about Sunday School, a new way of preparing the Sunday school lesson, creative teaching ideas, ways to think about growing a class, and how to reach out for new members and reach in to old members.

Marriage Ministry: A Guidebook
Bo Prosser & Charles Qualls

This book is equally helpful for ministers, for nearly/newlywed couples, and for thousands of couples across our land looking for fresh air in their marriages.

Music Ministry: A Guidebook
Donald Clark Measels, ed.

This work is an introduction to church music administration that provides insight into the responsibilities and demands placed on the person who heads the music program of a church.

Visit us online at **www.helwys.com/helpbooks** for helpful topics

CPSIA information can be obtained
at www.ICGtesting.com
Printed in the USA
LVOW04s1109281215

468085LV00019B/165/P